CREATIVE ORCHESTRATION

A Project Method for Classes in
Orchestration and Instrumentation

GEORGE F. McKAY
Professor of Music
University of Washington

Second Edition

Allyn and Bacon, Inc., Boston

To my wife, Frances,
for valiant assistance,
and to my colleagues and the
many students who have shared with
me the adventure of experience
and discussion from which this
theory of orchestration
gradually emerged.

Library of Congress
Catalog Card Number: 69-11499

Printed in the United States of America

PREFACE

THE ORCHESTRAL SOUNDS SUMMONED UP BY THE GEN-
iuses of music sometimes seem like sheer magic, but the
imagination and flair of the master composer must inevitably be
based upon certain principles of tonal relationship and procedure
which are the same for both the student beginner and the developed artist. Clear and effective sound and structure stem from
applications of unity, contrast and variety. These applications can
be formulated into fundamental types of technique which can be
understood and utilized by every student of music. The main
purpose of this book is to formulate a general theory based on
such techniques.

There have been too few theoretical speculations on orchestration by the composers of the past. Much has been written
by theorists about the technicalities of instrumentation, but far
too little has been said by the creative artists themselves about
"how" to write for the orchestra. The pioneering effort by Berlioz,
Treatise on Instrumentation, is lively and evocative and, in spite
of a certain obsolescence, still has much to offer from an artist's
creative insight. The modern revision by Richard Strauss has
further values derived from Strauss's own experienced craftsmanship.

Rimsky-Korsakov, in his *Principles of Orchestration,* offered
many creative suggestions, but fell short of a complete general
theory. Richard Wagner began his book *On Conducting* with
the sentence, "The secret of good orchestral sound is sustained
tone." With this fragmentary statement we are left groping at

unfulfilled total analysis because there are so many other sources of "good orchestral sound."

Sibelius has been quoted as saying, "The orchestra has no pedal." He meant that while improvising on the piano, use of the pedal produces a continuous resonance that can be had in the orchestra only by adding actual supplementary sustaining material. This is also strikingly true, but again, we are left groping toward a complete system which will surround all mastery of craftsmanship with basic explanation. It is toward such a complete, inclusive and far-reaching analysis of "how" to write "good" orchestration that this treatise is directed.

The methods of orchestration discussed in these pages, with their emphases upon central principles of effective sound and performance by small ensembles, were developed through many years of experience in teaching orchestration.

At first, standard books were used for reference and in teaching, but these were found to have an overemphasis on factual material and not enough discussion and illustration of the "how" and "why" of good orchestration.

Later, a method was adopted which emphasized the imitation of styles of various master composers. To learn orchestration the student was asked to analyze the scores of Bach, Mozart, Tchaikovsky, Debussy, etc., and to imitate these principal styles by writing full-score examples. This was a better method and led to much effective technic and the gradual formulation of a general theory. Eventually this method was also abandoned because, in writing for full orchestra, actual performance was too difficult to obtain; as a result, knowledge had to remain too theoretical. Furthermore, the student was usually impelled too strongly toward imitation; and his own individuality too often left dormant.

Finally, through further experiments in teaching, it became clear that the best results came from a freely creative use of general theory. The most creative orchestration occurred when the student was unburdened from imitating masterworks and was allowed to develop personal expression restricted only by the most fundamental guiding principles and by the sincere artistic criticism of an interested teacher.

Of all the musical studies, orchestration can be the most adventurous. But its ultimate sense of creativity can be had only if that which is written can be tried out in actual performance.

All the formulations contained in this book can be tried out successfully on a small ensemble of the type usually available among members of an orchestration class. (See page 295 for an example of a laboratory-type ensemble used at the University of Washington.) It is not necessary to write only for the large orchestra. The basic principles of clear organization and tonal interest are essentially the same for ten instruments as for one hundred. The large orchestra does have its uniquely full sound and the thrilling power that comes from the many players on each voice in the string section. The larger and more powerful the sound, the more there will be a need for clear organization to prevent blurring and confusion.

In forming an orchestra for which to write, it is best to have some representation of each family of sound (e.g., two woodwinds, one brass instrument, a few strings, a piano or other percussion) or some combination that will make available two or more choirs of sound (three woodwinds, four strings and piano, for instance). Any available small combination of mixed instruments will provide, for the student, much basic experience in the application of general principles. By writing for small groups, much time will be saved and the experience gained can later be applied to writing for the large orchestra.

Complete knowledge is a combination of theory with practical and artistic experience. Live performance of students' compositions is urgently necessary. In a day-by-day adventure in joint discovery the teacher can play a decisively creative role as analyst, critic and enthusiast. Now and then genius will appear in a few measures, and with it will come an exhilarating group feeling of identification with musical creativity.

This treatise, then, offers (1) complete information about the instruments of the orchestra—knowledge of their potentialities and limitations; (2) a comprehensive general theory; (3) a teaching method strongly motivated by emphasis upon creativity; (4) a practical means for testing results by actual performance; (5) an orderly and progressive study plan; (6) analytical discussion which stresses contemporaneity and musical frontiers; (7) principles of value to listener and conductor; (8) charts citing specific pages in standard scores where further illustrations may be found (see pages 301–303).

After using the first edition of *Creative Orchestration* in their classes many teachers felt that because the beginning student is so immensely curious about the various instruments (registers, ranges, timbres and technical problems), teaching method should stress a longer introductory period of making acquaintance with the separate instruments. Accordingly, this new expanded edition contains much more complete material on the instruments and it is suggested that beginning classes could spend considerable time writing small compositions for each of the instruments for a wealth of class demonstration of instrumental characteristics and possibilities.

Also, before going on to the creative projects more time needs to be spent on the basic problem of spacing out harmonic content. Project 1, consistency of unit organization, has therefore been greatly expanded with many special assignments that will give a thorough preparatory experience in harmonic organization.

An expression of appreciation is due the many interested teachers who wrote letters containing constructive suggestions. They have had a creative part in the shaping of this new edition.

George F. McKay

CONTENTS

Sufficient Instrumental Motion; Sufficient Vigor of Design; Sufficient Overlapping of Choirs; "Light and Shade" through Variegation of "Thickness and Thinness" of Texture; Sufficient Variety within General Design.

The Pre-Classic or Baroque Orchestra; The Classical Orchestra; The Modern Orchestra; The Expanded Orchestra; The Chamber Orchestra.

PLATES

PROJECTS

1

The Instruments
of the Orchestra

BEFORE YOU CAN WRITE CORRECTLY AND EFFECTIVELY
for the instruments of the orchestra, you will need to
know: (1) the ranges of the instruments, (2) how to write
for the instrumental parts which must be transposed (higher or
lower than actual sound), (3) something about the special qualities of different pitch locales or registers of each instrument, (4)
how to mark *staccato* and *legato* indications for wind instruments, and bowings for strings, (5) how to set the instruments
into effective motion, (6) how to avoid writing musical parts
which would be physically awkward or impossible for a player
to perform on his instrument and (7) how to write for each of
the instruments to bring forth the most effective and idiomatic
sound and motion.

The charts, examples and discussions which follow will
supply needed practical information together with concentrated
experiential knowledge to guide the beginner in his first attempts.

Before going on to the creative projects (page 127) it will
be most valuable and important to have much actual experience
with the various instruments. Whenever possible, performers
should be brought into the orchestration class to demonstrate
the typical idiomatic values of each of the instruments and to

illustrate ranges, registers, tonal characteristics and physical limitations.

Preparatory to the creative projects, and to bring the student still closer to the live meaning and value of each of the instruments, there will be a series of preliminary assignments. After the discussion of each separate instrument the student will be asked to write or arrange a short solo composition or passage which is typically idiomatic for the instrument. This will then be performed and critically analyzed within the orchestration class.

A second preparatory stage, related to acquaintance with the instruments, will be the writing or arranging for the separate families of instruments, each in turn (woodwinds, brass, percussion and strings). This will provide a first experience with the ordinary practicalities of register, range and spacing within each of the groups. These preparatory assignments, illustrating different ways of scoring the same music, will be found on page 106 as extensions of Project 1 (consistency of unit organization).

REGISTERS (actual sound)

Each instrument has characteristically different qualities— expressive timbres in high, low and middle registers. The following chart illustrates these areas. To know the extreme outer limits of range possibility, consult the special chart included in the discussion of each separate instrument.

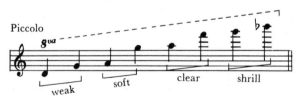

TRANSPOSITION RATIOS

In order to produce a correct pitch which will correspond with the rest of the orchestra, certain instrumental parts must be written higher or lower than the pitch or key in which the rest of the orchestra is playing.

In the chart below, the natural pitch of each of these transposing instruments is compared to middle C. To determine how much higher or lower to write the part for a specified instrument, find the interval listed for it on the transposition chart below.

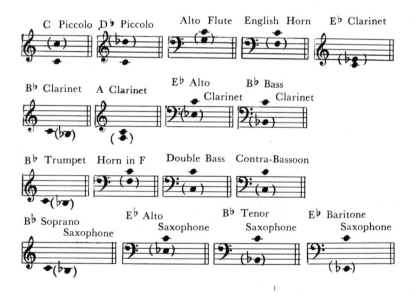

TRANSPOSITION CHART

CAUTION: *Although alto flute, English horn, French horn, and the lower clarinets and saxophones play partially in bass*

7

register, the orchestra part must always be written in treble clef. Only double bass and contra-bassoon will be written in bass clef.

If middle C is *lower* than the pitch tone (the tone in parenthesis), the part for that instrument must be written *lower* than actual sound by the distance shown.

If middle C is *higher* than the pitch tone of the instrument, the part must be written *higher* than actual sound by the distance shown.

For instance, the chart shows that for the C piccolo, middle C is an octave *lower* than the pitch tone. The part must therefore be written an octave *lower* than actual sound. For the horn in F the chart shows that middle C is a fifth *higher* than the pitch tone. The part must therefore be written a fifth *higher* than actual sound.

If you want a B-flat clarinet to sound as follows

the part would have to be written a whole step higher:

If you want a horn in F to sound

the part must be written a fifth higher:

When a part is transposed, the key signatures are also changed by the same ratio as the notes for the part.

The B-flat clarinet part above has been transposed up a whole step. Transposition of the key of C up a whole step makes the addition of the two sharps in the signature necessary in order to indicate the key of D major.

The traditional practice in transposing for the horn has been to dispense with key signatures and mark in all needed sharps and flats. Although the horn is still out of step with the general practice for transposition, some composers are now beginning to use key signatures in the horn part.

METHODS OF TONE PRODUCTION

Although electronic means of tone production have now become an important part of general musical practice, the traditional methods of tone production seem to be unshakably established as basic means of producing tonal variety. From remotest antiquity to the present day, musical sounds have resulted from

1. Blowing across the open end of a pipe (a relatively weak sound limited to instruments such as the ancient *syrinx* and *pan pipes*).

2. Blowing across a circular hole bored into a pipe (all flutes of differing sizes use this principle).

3. Blowing into a whistle-type mouthpiece (the revival of the instruments of the recorder family has brought this principle back into usage in recent music).

9

4. Setting a single reed into motion against a solid surface as wind is blown into a cylindrical pipe (clarinets and saxophones).

5. Setting two reeds into motion, vibrating against one another as wind is blown into a conical pipe (oboes and bassoons).

6. Blowing directly into a length of tubing but using the lips as the vibrating medium (all brass instruments).

7. Strings set into vibration by a bow drawn across them (violin, viola, cello, and double bass).

8. Strings set into vibration by plucking (all viol-type instruments and the harpsichord, mandolin, guitar, etc.).

9. Strings set into vibration by striking (the piano and such early or folk instruments as the *dulcimer* or *cimbalom*).

10. Hollow resonators of indefinite pitch resonated by striking or shaking (drums, tambourines, various gourd types).

11. Hollow resonators of definite pitch (timpani, temple blocks).

12. Solid resonators of indefinite pitch (cymbals, triangle, etc.).

13. Solid resonators of definite pitch (celesta, glockenspiel, marimba, xylophone, vibraharp).

14. Various means set into vibration by an electric current (Theremin, Martenot, Hammond organ).

THE ORDER OF INSTRUMENTS IN SCORING

An examination of modern scores will show an unvarying order for the placing of the families of instruments in the score. Woodwinds are always at the top, with the highest-sounding instruments first and lowest-sounding instruments last. Using pitch as a criterion the woodwinds are placed in this order:

Piccolo
Flutes
Alto Flute

Oboes

English Horn

Clarinets

Bass Clarinet

Bassoon

Contra-bassoon

Directly below the woodwinds will be the choir of French Horns, usually

Horns 1 and 2

Horns 3 and 4

Next will come the brass instruments of the trumpet-trombone-tuba family.

Trumpets

Trombones

Tuba

Below the brass grouping will come any keyboard sound or voice choir.

Piano

Celesta

Harpsichord

Harp

If both voices and keyboard instrument are used, the keyboard instrument would be below the voices to coordinate it in spacing by visual nearness to the percussion instruments.

Next will come the staves for percussion instruments.

Finally, at the bottom of the score there will be the string choir with all string instruments arranged in natural order of pitch.

First Violins

Second Violins

Violas

Cellos

Double Bass

This specific order of instruments in the score is said to have evolved to accommodate the normal action of the eye as it sweeps the page from bottom to top. The strings traditionally carry most of the meaningful structure and are therefore placed at the bottom of the page so as to be easier to find and follow. The woodwinds, traditionally of next importance, are at the top, and the brass and percussion, with more subsidiary relation to the total structure, are at the center. This order was not always in vogue and many deviations can be found in earlier scores, but all contemporary conductors have long since become used to the order expounded here and for best rehearsal results it should be followed systematically.

If an exotic or ancient instrument like the recorder or *viola da gamba* is used, it should be included at the proper pitch relation to the family in which it appears or should be set apart in a separate staff just above the family to which it belongs. Placement would depend upon the relation of such an unusual instrument to the texture. If it is to be heard as a solo voice independent from a harmonic body, it would be set apart from the main choir. If it is to be a part of the harmonic effect, it would be included within the body of sound.

In planning the use of staves on a page of written score, always leave one staff open between families of sound so that the eye can easily single out the several groups.

WOODWIND INSTRUMENTS

The first woodwind instruments were pipes or reeds with holes bored into them. The holes were spaced at distances needed to produce the typical scales of primitive music. These early instruments must have been either badly out of tune or difficult to play because to cover the holes effectively the player had to cope with very strenuous fingering problems caused by uneven distances and awkward hand positions. If the holes had been bored to accommodate the hand, the instrument would have been out of tune.

The modern Boehm system of keys, extension bars, pads and levers has changed all this. The holes can now be bored at exactly the right point in the pipe for perfected intonation and the instrument can be played with fluency and economy of motion.

Since the perfection of the keys and levers is a relatively recent development, the importance of the woodwinds in scoring is also relatively recent. Scores by early classic composers show the woodwinds in a rather restricted role with much doubling of the strings, which were then the principal choir of the orchestra.

As the mechanical problems of playing the woodwind instruments were gradually solved, it became apparent that their naturally exciting agility and variety of timbre made them especially suited to melodic and foreground use. In the works of Debussy, Ravel, and Stravinsky the woodwinds came into their own, with strings often relegated to a supporting background while woodwinds were featured as melodic foreground.

To experience this emphasis on the woodwinds as foreground, listen to the later works of Debussy, especially *La Mer* and *Iberia*, and to *Daphnis et Chloé* by Ravel. Also analyze the three famous ballet suites by Stravinsky, *The Firebird*, *Petrouchka*, and *Le Sacre du printemps*, to observe the interaction between woodwinds and strings.

In addition to the use of woodwinds as foreground, you will also hear woodwind motion at its imaginative best, and you will become aware of the timbre vividness of the higher and lower registers of the woodwinds and the relatively weak and uncharacteristic sound of the middle registers.

As you study the woodwind action in these extraordinary scores you will come to see how important motor action and kinesthetic values are to woodwind writing. Somehow the harmonies are less important to woodwind values than to brass or keyboard instruments, for instance. Woodwinds tend to make a dull effect unless there is sufficient kinesthetic interest (typical instrumental motion). The following chart shows in compact form some of the general types of woodwind motion.

Woodwind Effects

Strings must constantly change bows in *legato* passages, whereas woodwinds can play *legato* passages on one breath, much as a singer does when singing a phrase.

In writing for the wind instruments, indicate the *staccato* and *legato* character by dots and slurs. Because winds are more sluggish in articulation than strings, any *staccato* effects in winds will have to be vividly indicated and you may have to add additional instructions to the *staccato* markings. Use descriptive terms such as "crisp," "emphatic," "delicate," "vigorous," etc.

Wind instruments can play quite long and continuous *legato* passages without too much trouble. *Legato* passages can be made most effective by shaping them in accordance with those points where the player would naturally pause for breath.

In writing woodwind parts mix *staccato* and *legato* vividly. Do not expect the player to play a *legato* passage that is too unreasonably long on one breath, and remember that every separated note must be tongued or started as though speaking the syllable "tu" or by a rapid alternation of "tu ku, tu ku," using tongue and throat.

The woodwinds differ somewhat in the matter of natural agility. Flute is the most agile, clarinet is the next most agile, bassoon is only moderately agile but has a superior natural *staccato* possibility. Oboe is best when limited to smaller amounts of *staccato* and agility demand, but has a superior power to project *legato* passages which have only a moderate degree of activity. Saxophones are moderately agile but a bit sluggish in *staccato*.

The elaborate fingering systems of the woodwinds make it desirable to take any difficult passage to a player for testing to see if it cannot be made more fluent by modifying it here and there to facilitate fingering and phrasing. However, the best players have amazing capabilities. With players of lesser skill, more caution must be exercised in difficult trills and awkward fingering.

Another general observation about the woodwinds is that when used in the full orchestra they tend to be the weakest family of sound and the beginning orchestrator will have to live through the actual playing of one of his orchestrations to fully realize this. Unless placed in vivid register or against a dull enough background the woodwinds tend to be obliterated and absorbed. Rimsky-Korsakov has observed that when a woodwind is doubled with a string choir it tends to be absorbed by the string tone, but adds a richer quality to the string effect.

This comparative weakness of the woodwinds is a further argument for sufficiently active design as a means of bringing the woodwind sound to the attention of the listener in competition with the rest of the orchestra.

When woodwinds are used harmonically, any reasonable or balanced grouping can have an attractive effect. Rimsky-Korsakov points out the superior effect of combining two instruments of one timbre with a single instrument of different timbre, e.g., two flutes and one oboe, or two clarinets and one bassoon, as opposed to three different instruments.

In the full orchestra the classic practice was to use woodwinds in groups of two, as in the following example (two flutes, two oboes, two clarinets, two bassoons):

Modern composers use groups of three to make up the woodwind choir (piccolo, two flutes; two oboes, English horn; two clarinets, bass clarinet; two bassoons, contra-bassoon):

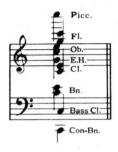

More complete explanation of harmonic spacing of woodwinds will be given in connection with the assignments in Project 1 (consistency of unit organization) (page 107–113).

Each of the woodwind instruments will now be discussed separately. The order of presentation will be the order in which they normally appear in the full score (woodwinds, brass, percussion, strings). We therefore begin with the piccolo and end with the double bass.

The Piccolo

Italian: *Flauto piccolo* (or *Ottavino*)
French: *Petite flûte*
German: *Kleine Flöte*

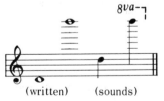

17

The piccolo extends the range of the flute up one octave. It also has its own expressive power and a timbre uniquely different from that of the flute. When brought in suddenly and briefly it makes a telling effect with its brilliant surprise. Its middle register is rather plain and does not cut through easily but in its highest register it is interestingly bright and shrill, even shockingly so. The lower register of the piccolo is somewhat weak but interestingly individual.

The most effective register is in the bright upper tone where the music is clear enough, relaxed enough and can be played with the most agility.

Since the piccolo most universally used is the piccolo in C, transposition requires no key change, but it must be written an octave lower than the actual sound desired. In other words, the piccolo always sounds an octave higher than the written part.

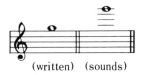

(written) (sounds)

A piccolo in D-flat is sometimes used in bands. In writing for the D-flat piccolo the part must be transposed a minor ninth lower and the key signature changed accordingly.

(sounds) (written)

In its extreme low register the piccolo is rather weak, but if used with very thin background it can make an unusual poetic effect, sweetly wan, gently expressive.

The piccolo is often used to reinforce the flute part. When it doubles in the octave it adds a bright edge to the flute timbre. When it is used as an actual doubling (written an octave lower than the flute) it is absorbed by the flute tone but adds to its power.

Since the fingering for the piccolo is exactly the same as for the flute, the player of second or third flute can also play the piccolo part by changing from one instrument to the other.

The only requirement is that the player be given time enough to change and adjust to the different size of embouchure.

The Flute

Italian: *Flauto, Flauti*
French: *Flûte, Flûtes*
German: *Flöte, Flöten*

The flute is a non-transposing instrument. The part for the flute is written exactly as it sounds. Although composers have written for the flute down to the low B

and as high as D.

These extremes are rather impracticable and risky. For practical purpose it is best to think of the flute range as a total of three registers, low, middle and high, each with its typical timbre encompassed by an octave.

The lower octave contains the rarest flute timbre. Here is found the appealing and evocative depth and primitive intensity that caused Debussy to begin his *Afternoon of a Faun* with a flute solo in that register.

When this choice timbre is used, the accompaniment must be delicate enough to allow it to sound through.

In its middle octave the flute is sweetly clear and relaxed and may give the illusion of being lower in sound than it actually is.

from GRIEG: *Peer Gynt*

In its highest octave the flute is brilliant, and would be used in that register when doubling for powerful effect, as in the orchestral *tutti*.

The notes from the highest A to the highest C are difficult to play. They must be used with caution and limited to *fortissimo* passages.

The dynamic capabilities of the flute are only moderate. It can play very softly but can never equal the special loudness of such instruments as the trumpet and timpani. This means that the orchestrator must be constantly aware of the amount of sound pitted against the flute, otherwise the flute tone may be obliterated or absorbed.

The flute player has to expend considerably more breath than do other wind players and therefore must have sufficient time to breathe and an occasional rest for the lips.

For technical reasons avoid the following trills.

All brass and woodwind instruments, due to the length of the pipe, have a basic pitch and certain natural overtones. The flute is fundamentally in D and would therefore have a certain natural predilection for music in that key and in related keys. However, the modern flute technic is so capable that this need not make much difference in choosing an orchestral key. With brasses and strings, choice of key is a more vital matter.

The flute tone contains the very essence of lyric feeling and pastoral poetry. It is ideally suited to melodic use, especially against a background of string tone. It is also particularly interesting in the active sort of design shown in the following excerpt.

FROM SCHUMANN SYMPHONY NO. 1

The Alto Flute

Italian: *Flauto contralto*
French: *Flûte en sol*
German: *Altflöte*

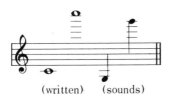

(written)   (sounds)

The alto flute is a transposing instrument. It is a flute in G and therefore the part must be written a fourth higher than it sounds. Its special use is as a stronger third part in passages using a trio of flutes. Since its character is that of a low or "alto" voice, its upper tones are of less consequence and not so easily distinguishable from the ordinary flute tone as are the lower tones. It is not as much different from the ordinary flute tone as viola is different from violin or as English horn is different from oboe, but it does have a deeper, darker, more substantial flute tone. Not every orchestra has an alto flute and the clarinet is often used as a substitute.

The Oboe

Italian: *Oboe, Oboi*
French: *Hautbois, Hautbois*
German: *Oboe, Oboen*

When well played, the oboe is unsurpassed for poignancy. Its intense and impassioned tone is ideal for use in simple melody and for the enrichment of other timbres by doubling. The oboist, more than any other player, needs time to breathe and prepare for entrances. *Staccato* articulation is more definite than on the flute, but must not be too rapid or lengthy. All simple *legato* passages sound well but should usually be kept within middle register, since the higher and lower registers are extremely intense in sound and more difficult to play. Rapidly moving accompaniment patterns do not seem suited to the character of the oboe, and skips from register to register should be limited to a few well prepared leaps.

The oboe does not transpose. Write the part for it exactly as it sounds.

Most of the part for the oboe should be within the more relaxed and normal-sounding middle register.

24

The most developed players are able to play all the tones of the low register, including the low B-flat, but this tone cannot be started without a quite positive attack and a rather loud tone. The low B-natural and C are more useful and secure.

The best players also get a good tone up to the high D or E-flat.

The difference in technical skill between the most professional players and those only moderately skilled is very marked. Therefore when writing for lesser players it is wise to keep the tones within a limited range and in the general area of the middle register.

It is here that most of the typically melodic passages for oboe are written. It is here that the player is most comfortable and the tone most appealingly effective.

from DVORAK: *Symphony No. 8*

In the lower register the tone rapidly takes on increased power, darkness and special dramatic intensity. A certain amount of florid *legato* motion seems to bring out the timbre of this register most vividly.

Above the high D there are tones which *can* be played but these should be used with great caution and written only for the very experienced player. Ordinarily these extreme high tones will be undesirably stringent and shrill.

Trills are possible but the complexities of fingering make it desirable to test out all trills and tremolos with a player and to modify those which do not work out or which awkwardly interrupt the musical context.

Keep most trills within the comfortable middle register and avoid all tremolos larger than a fourth above the tone E.

Two rare special effects may be experimented with. The oboe may be played with flutter-tongue (but not as easily as flute or clarinet) and also muted by stuffing the bell with a handkerchief or cork. The muting changes the tone only slightly through a softening of impact and this applies mainly to lower register.

Because of the delicate control required to produce the tone, the need to hold back the breath while exerting unusual pressure and the necessity of starting each new passage with a very positive attack by tonguing, the oboe is one of the most difficult of all instruments. With the exception, perhaps, of the horn, the oboe needs the most rest between difficult passages and the most consideration toward its problems of attack and entry.

Because the tone quality of the oboe is so extraordinarily characteristic, its most telling effect is when it enters as a new timbre and does not continue for too long. The oboe is at its best as a magnificent melodic instrument, and in this role is nearly always heard alone against some suitable background.

27

from SCHUBERT: *Unfinished Symphony*

When used within the body of orchestral sound for harmonic effect, the oboe intervals will usually stay within the less stringent timbre of middle register for a better blend with other woodwinds. For special harmonic effect, two oboes combined with English horn (alto oboe) in the low register make a most interesting and vital harmonic timbre.

Because the oboe timbre is the very archetype of pointed, biting and edged sound, it combines wonderfully with any opposing timbre (oboe and flute; oboe and horn; oboe and violin) and is often used for such doubling or tone mixing.

For illustration of typical oboe writing hear the slow movement, *Symphony in C* by Bizet or *The Winter's Past* by Barlow. A rarity is the use of bass oboe in *A Dance Rhapsody* by Delius.

28

The English Horn

Italian: *Corno inglese*
French: *Cor anglais*
German: *Englisches Horn*

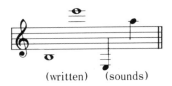

(written)   (sounds)

The English horn (also very commonly known as *cor anglais*) is an alto oboe. Its range and general technical problems are similar to those of the oboe but it is basically in F instead of C. It is a transposing instrument and the part for it must be written a fifth higher than it is to sound.

The English horn sounds best in its middle register, where its deeply brooding and pungently dark timbre can be most easily produced. The higher and lower registers are stringent and cannot be played softly. The tone is phenomenally expressive and attractive but must be used sparingly. In its essentially melodic role, the English horn is most valuable for the expression of the more tragic and meditative moods. It also adds a choice richness when used as an alto voice in woodwind harmony.

The actual sound extends down to the low E.

In the following melodic passage the English horn is limited to the middle register.

(written)   (sounds)

The English horn may be thought of as slightly more ponderous in motion than the oboe, and it is naturally a shade slower in its articulation and attack.

To furnish complete harmonic resources within the woodwind choir, fully developed orchestras will usually have three separate players; first oboe, second oboe and English horn. When there are only two oboe players the second oboist can usually play the English horn part by changing instruments at the point where English horn is specified.

Since the English horn player is a specialist in low timbre, his technic will be fluent in the lowest register.

Another alto oboe type that will sometimes be found is the Oboe d' amore in A.

(actual sound)

A use of bass oboe or heckelphone can be heard in *A Dance Rhapsody* by Delius, where it is used both as a solo instrument and as a member of the harmonic grouping of oboe sounds.

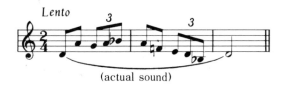

(actual sound)

Oboe, English Horn, and Bass Oboe

later

(actual sound)

In this work a sarrusophone is also specified and there is an opportunity to compare the tone of the bass oboe (heckelphone) with that of the sarrusophone (a contra-bassoon type with a metal body).

The Clarinet

Italian: *Clarinetto, Clarinetti*
French: *Clarinette, Clarinettes*
German: *Klarinette, Klarinetten*

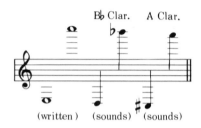

(written)   (sounds)   (sounds)

There are several sizes of clarinets, each of which is identified by a basic pitch. There are clarinets in E-flat, B-flat, and A; there is also an alto clarinet in E-flat, and a bass clarinet in B-flat. The B-flat clarinet is the one most commonly used, and its liquid tone has a sweet, warm, expressiveness. The A clarinet has the same flexibility as the B-flat but its tonal character is darker and more tragic.

The shrill, gay and prankish E-flat clarinet is garishly high in pitch and is rarely used except for special dramatic effect and tonal grotesquerie. The B-flat bass clarinet has a particularly dark and deep tone.

Clarinets are very motile. Clarinetists are able to skip about easily from high to low register and, like flutists, can easily execute runs and rapidly moving *legato* designs. They can also maintain a sustained tone or a slow *legato*. As on the flute, *staccato* articulation will be played with sufficient definiteness only when specially marked with dots and interpretative indications: e.g., "incisive," "delicate," *marcato*, etc.

In its middle register the B-flat clarinet is disappointingly weak and relatively characterless. In its upper tones it becomes strikingly bright and powerful, while in the *chalumeau* or low register it has an unequalled rich, mellow, deep quality much treasured for its poetic power. The extreme high notes must be used with caution because of a disagreeable shrillness that increases markedly as the player approaches the top of the range.

Outstanding illustration of clarinet use can be heard in the *Première rhapsodie* for clarinet and orchestra by Debussy or *Quintet* for clarinet and strings by Brahms. The prankish E-flat clarinet can be heard in *Concertino* for piano and orchestra by Janáček, in *Till Eulenspiegels lustige Streiche* by Strauss, and in *El Salón México* by Copland. Bass clarinet can be heard in "Dance of the Sugar Plum Fairy" from the Tchaikovsky *Nutcracker Suite*.

The professional clarinetist must have two instruments, one in B-flat and the other in A. For ease in playing music in flat keys, the score will specify B-flat clarinet. This will cut down the number of accidentals in the player's parts. If the music is in sharp keys, the composer will indicate clarinet in A for the same reason.

These two differently pitched clarinets also differ in dramatic feeling. For warm, sunny music, B-flat clarinet might be specified. For darker, more tragic meaning, it would be more effective to turn to the clarinet in A.

All the commonly used clarinets are transposing instruments. The B-flat clarinet must be written a whole step higher than the sound desired and the key signature changed accordingly. The A clarinet must be written a minor third higher than actual sound. The E-flat clarinet must be written a minor third lower than actual sound. The E-flat alto clarinet is written a major sixth higher than actual sound.

The bass clarinet is most often in B-flat but occasionally has been scored as a clarinet in A.

(written)　　　(sounds)

Some scores (German) show the bass clarinet written in bass clef with the part for the B-flat bass clarinet transposed up a whole step and the bass clarinet in A transposed up a minor third higher than actual sound. But the general practice in conformance with standard procedure shows the bass clarinet in B-flat transposed a major ninth higher and always in treble clef, and the bass clarinet in A transposed a minor tenth higher and in treble clef. Use this more modern system.

(sounds)　　　(written)

Still other sizes of clarinet are mentioned in the most technically exhaustive listings. For practical purpose the clarinets in D and C (sopranino—higher than the standard B-flat clarinet), the so-called basset horn (an alto clarinet in F) and the contrabass clarinet in B-flat (an octave lower than the standard bass clarinet) will only be mentioned in passing. The detailed discussion will be given to those clarinets most commonly found in existing orchestras.

The B-flat clarinet may be thought of as the standard

clarinet. It brings out typical register differences in a more vivid way than other clarinets.

The range of the B-flat clarinet is admirably wide. Four differing registers can be singled out for comment. The *chalumeau* or low register (from B-flat below middle C down to the D a sixth below) is marvelously rich and deep.

(actual sound)

From B-flat up to about G, a sixth above (the so-called "break"), the tone is less characterful and suited only to uses where a neutral and relatively weak tone is wanted.

Above the "break" the tone changes to a more vivid and silvery bright character. This area extends roughly up to C above the staff.

From there on up, the tones become increasingly shrill, stringent and risky for ordinary use.

35

The high E-flat clarinet is an instrument used especially for humor and characterization. Its entertaining high register timbre is usually featured. Its low register is of less interest.

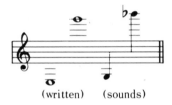

(written)   (sounds)

The bass clarinet is unimpressive in its higher registers but is magnificently deep and darkly authentic in its lower register.

It can be used for tonal surprise in its low register, and it adds vital reinforcing power when doubled with low strings, bassoon, or tuba. The bass clarinet should carry melody only briefly, because of its intensely vivid roundness and substantial tone. Like all low instruments, it must articulate and move more slowly. The bass clarinet has the most authentic depth of all instrumental timbres, and its use could well be restricted to its deep low and middle registers. The upper tones are more difficult to play and are somewhat dry and grotesque in effect. The E-flat alto clarinet is known mainly as a moderately deep timbre which adds mellowness and depth to woodwind harmony.

The clarinets are the most naturally *legato* of all the instruments and can make almost all trills with relative ease. The tone is very round, liquid and smooth; it is the natural antithesis to all the more raucous and pointed sounds, and is therefore of special value in tone blending.

The clarinet *staccato* is a little less natural than the *staccato* of flute, oboe, or bassoon, and therefore must be positively articulated and clearly indicated by the structure of the music and the markings. The following examples illustrate the typical kinesthetic values of clarinet motion.

from MENDELSSOHN: *Fingal's Cave*

from WAGNER: *Tannhäuser*

37

The dynamic possibilities include easy manipulation of softness and loudness, from the most imperceptible softness to quite strident and penetrating sounds in the upper register.

When used within the woodwind choir for harmonic purpose, the clarinet blends best when used in its least conspicuous registers; but many conscious exceptions to this rule will be found.

Larger professional orchestras will usually have three clarinetists (first clarinet, second clarinet and bass clarinet). Smaller orchestras are likely to have only two players. In this situation, the score can instruct the second clarinetist to discontinue the second clarinet part and take up the bass clarinet at a specified point.

In situations where all three players are available, it is best to use the bass clarinet sparingly in its role as third part in harmonic formations. It is such a heavy sound that too much use can become wearing to the listener. Its authentic depth makes it a valuable means of strengthening the bass line occasionally, but its very different and dominating timbre makes it an essentially melodic instrument and its principal use should be for moments of melodic foreground.

The Bassoon

Italian: *Fagotto, Fagotti*
French: *Basson, Bassons*
German: *Fagott, Fagotte*

The bassoon has a timbre of great individuality. It has a certain ungainly charm that lends itself to comic effects, but it can also be plaintively expressive, especially in the upper part of its range.

One use of the bassoon is as a thickening ingredient for the bass in passages where fullness and power are needed. When used as foreground or melody its value is mainly in the addition of dramatic characterization. Because of the grotesque character of its sound the listener's interest is soon lost when the soloistic bassoon timbre is overused.

The bassoonist can make skips with relative ease, and *legato* playing is possible but does not sound quite as comfortably fluent as on the flute or the clarinet. As with the oboe, florid design goes somewhat "against the grain," but *staccato* effects are very natural and are easily produced.

The bassoon may disappoint if expected to sound softly in the lowest register. As the player progresses down into this register there is an increasingly sharp edge to the articulation that works against the possibility of playing softly.

The bassoon is a non-transposing instrument. Write the

39

part exactly as it sounds. As it moves into its highest register, the part should be written in the tenor clef to avoid too many high ledger lines.

(sounds)   (written)

This upper register is particularly plaintive and appealing. Therefore most bassoonists cultivate the upper register and are able to play fluently and expressively within it.

from BEETHOVEN: *Symphony No. 5*.

The middle register is rather easily covered due to its more relaxed and less characteristic tone.

The lower octave, as has already been pointed out, is gruff and penetrating. To modify this rather harsh power, a handkerchief is sometimes stuffed into the bell.

The fingering system of the bassoon is still less mechanically perfect than that of some other instruments. It is said that to preserve the typical bassoon timbre it has been necessary to retain some primitiveness of mechanism. Tremolos can be played, but it is best to avoid those wider than a fourth. Certain trills are impossible, and it is best to test the trills out with players before including them in the score.

The bassoon timbre mixes very well with the strings and gives a particularly mellow result when combined in unison with viola or cello. For special melodic variety, classic composers often doubled the violin melody with the bassoon an octave lower.

The harmonic role of the bassoon will be dealt with at length in the discussion of unit structure (page 107–117).

For typical examples of bassoon use, hear the very opening measures of *Le Sacre du printemps* by Stravinsky, the opening statement of *L'Apprenti sorcier* by Dukas, and the beginning of the movement "Uranus" from *The Planets* by Holst.

Study these illustrations of typical bassoon motion.

Saint-Säens. Danse Macabre

from DVORAK: *Symphony No. 8*

There is a still lower bassoon, the contra-bassoon.

It is pitched an octave below the bassoon. The part must be transposed up one octave.

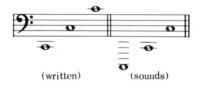

Because its tone is somewhat dull and harsh, and its action necessarily sluggish, it is mainly useful for octave doubling to create the deepest possible bass effects, but it is occasionally used for special dramatic characterization: e.g., to represent the beast in "Beauty and the Beast" from the *Mother Goose Suite* by Ravel.

There is also a metal type contra-bassoon known as the sarrusophone. Of the several sizes of sarrusophone it is the contra-bass sarrusophone in C that would serve this purpose. Its register is as follows.

Like the contra-bassoon, its part must be written an octave higher than actual sound.

The Saxophone

Italian: *Sassofono, Sassofoni*
French: *Saxophone, Saxophones*
German: *Saxophon, Saxophone*

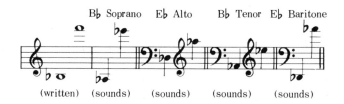

Like the clarinet, the saxophone is available in several sizes, each with its own characteristic pitch and timbre. The differences of tone quality within the saxophone family are less marked than those within the clarinet family.

43

The E-flat alto is the standard saxophone. It is relaxed and normal in its sound, whereas the B-flat soprano instrument is rather nasal and grotesquely high in sound. The B-flat tenor saxophone has a nobler depth and a certain heaviness, while the E-flat baritone has an especially deep resonance which can add an illusion of substance and rich depth to woodwind harmony. A feature of the saxophone is a certain uniformity of quality throughout its range.

The saxophone is somewhat handicapped by a relatively sluggish articulation and a certain regularity of tone quality that works against variety of dynamics and register. In small groups it tends to be garishly prominent, but in the large orchestra it tends to disappear into the generality of the full sound without adding much to its character. It does have certain unique soloistic expressive potentialities and has been used for a certain soft richness of tone—as in Bizet's *L'Arlésienne* suite; for a high festive brilliance—as in Ravel's *Bolero*; and to characterize a certain mawkish wistfulness—as in Prokofiev's *Lieutenant Kijé*.

The saxophones are transposing instruments. The B-flat soprano is written a whole step higher than actual sound, the E-flat alto a major sixth higher, the B-flat tenor is written a major ninth higher—always in treble clef and with corresponding change of key signature.

The approximate registers are shown in the chart on page 4.

BRASS INSTRUMENTS

The modern brass instruments are descended from primitive types associated with hunting and war. Some of the vigor and power of these early instruments still remains, and a certain directness and startling impact are still natural to brass sound.

The modern mechanical improvements of brass instruments through fingering mechanisms and slides, the invention of mutes and the gradual evolution of more positive timbre differentiations within the family of brass instruments have opened up extraordinary new brass potentialities. Brasses need no longer be limited to the crudely simple designs of the natural horns and trumpets of the classic composers (although a certain stark naturalness and dignity may still be had from such simplicity and openness).

If he will avoid the stringencies of the most extreme registers, and give sufficient time for recovery after a difficult passage and sufficient preparation for new entry, the composer can call upon the brasses for almost any reasonable *staccato* and *legato* design. The brasses have been too long thought of as essentially *staccato* or "fanfare" instruments. They are especially interesting in *legato* design and this may be thought of as a frontier for experimentation. There are still some physical limitations (these will be explained in the detailed discussion of each instrument) but these are less restricting than they formerly were. Essentially, the composer has to decide whether he wants to exploit the drama of the ancient or primitive brass character, or move out into pure design and liberated motion.

The brass sound can be divided into three main categories. The "warm" brass (the French horns), the "mellow" brass (cornets, baritone horn, tuba), and the "clear" brass (the trumpets). The trombones are somewhere in between the "clear" brass and the "mellow" brass and the tone can be produced to contribute to either timbre ideal, but the trombones

45

are usually working in partnership with the trumpets as an extension of the "clear" brass family and in contrast with the horns (the "warm" brass). The cornets and the "mellow" brass timbres have been brought into the orchestra only occasionally and experimentally. Bizet used cornets in the opera *Carmen* instead of trumpets. Franck used both cornets and trumpets in his famous *Symphony in D minor*.

The fundamental timbre differences seem to result from the differing combinations of tubing length with size and shape of the bell. The horn has a very long and narrow tubing combined with comparatively sudden and extremely wide flaring of the bell.

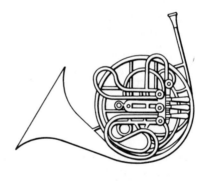

"Warm" brass.

The trumpet has a tube length that is relatively shorter than that of the French horn and a more sudden but less wide bell.

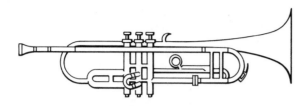

"Clear" brass.

The cornet, baritone and tuba have the same relative tubing length as the trumpet but a more gradual flaring of the bell.

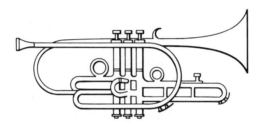

"Mellow" brass.

The brass section of the orchestra, then, seems to have evolved into a resource richly multiple through its ability to sound the different timbres either separately (antiphonally) or with the blended sound of the full brass section.

In the modern brass choir there is also a tendency toward the widening of the total range, resulting in a more vivid register differentiation.

From the listener's standpoint the brass is a rather intense experience, and must therefore be used somewhat sparingly. Berlioz in the *Symphonie Fantastique* saves his brass so as to make an extremely dramatic impact when it enters. In the opposite direction, however, Skalkottas in his *Greek Dances* uses

47

the brass as a principal sound and the strings as the supplementary timbre (reversing the normal procedure).

In his treatise on instrumentation, Rimsky-Korsakov gives a scale of intensities in accordance with the theory that the more intense the experience the less bearable it is over long periods of time. The percussions and bell sounds are the most intense and therefore must be used the most sparingly. Next in intensity are the brasses, then the woodwinds. Finally, the strings have the least intensity and may be used for the longest periods of time without becoming wearing.

If Rimsky-Korsakov's theory is valid, then there would be a parallel scale of intensities within the brass section. The extreme registers would be the most intense; the middle registers less intense. The "clear" brass (trumpet–trombone choir) would therefore be more intense than the "warm" brass (choir of horns). The horns should be used at greater length and more often than the trumpets and trombones, and middle registers at greater length than extreme registers.

Another of Rimsky-Korsakov's general rules that may well be taken into account is that in playing *mf* it will take two horns to balance one trumpet or one trombone. Unless this balance is applied, the dynamic markings must be adjusted accordingly.

Mutes make an astonishing difference in the dynamic power of the brass instruments. Unmuted they are the most dominating of timbres, but muted they become quite weak and care must be taken in writing or marking surrounding timbres so that the muted brasses are not obliterated.

Of all the melodic voices of the orchestra, the brasses have the most striking potentiality for dynamic variation. They can play *pp* or *ff* and make the gradation from one to the other with relative ease; also much can be made of dynamic effects such as *sfz* and *fp* marked accentings, sudden *crescendo*, sudden *diminuendo* and other dynamically inventive markings.

If the composer wishes to stress the natural idiomatic

differences of the woodwind, brass and strings, the brass will naturally move at a slower pace than either the woodwind or strings; but when the order is reversed for special effect (brass moving faster than woodwind or strings), or when the brass enters with a sudden flurry of rapid motion, it will have an especially striking impact due to the excitement created by an element of surprise.

Brasses can play flutter-tongue marked as follows.

Because they are each based on a length of tubing which has a strongly resonant set of natural tones based on the natural overtone series, brass instruments have pedal tones (fundamental tones below the tones available in the fingering and slide systems). If articulated successfully, these can be used for special effect. Pedal tones of each of the instruments will be discussed in the special sections devoted to them.

Because of the vividly consonant individuality given to the brasses by the strong resonance of their natural overtones, they may be considered to be a medium naturally adapted to the projection of harmonic values. They ring out the full glory of consonant harmony, but because of their inherently consonant resonance they also add great richness and glamor to dissonant harmonies.

In spite of the excellence of technic of most modern professional brass players, a few physical difficulties remain. The instrument must still be periodically drained of moisture and time must be allowed for this in long compositions. Because a great deal of breath must usually be expended, the playing of brass instruments is strenuous and rest periods are important. The extreme

49

high and low registers still require great skill and it is best not to expect a player to strike a very high note suddenly and play it *p* or *pp*. Experience with brasses will quickly make the orchestrator conscious of the very great differences involved in the different registers and he will become acutely aware and cautious about the shakiness of the few highest tones. They can be played, but there must be suitable preparation, an effective context, and motion and duration that are not too taxing.

The few lowest tones are also somewhat problematical and must be approached carefully and used infrequently.

The following chart shows some of the generalities of the motion of brass instruments.

Brass Effects

Mutes   Straight mute (standard)
Cardboard mute
Cup mute
Harmon mute
Metal mute
"Jazz" mute
Robinson mute etc.

Off-stage

(muted effect)

The Horn

Italian: *Corno, Corni*
French: *Cor, Cors*
German: *Horn, Hörner*

(written)   (sounds)

The modern French horn is a transposing instrument which is written a fifth higher than it sounds. The original horn was founded on only one pitch, but most horns now are double horns (so called). Through the addition of extra tubing, the player is enabled to play as though playing on either a F horn or upon a horn in B-flat. This gives a wider choice of fingerings to facilitate production of tone and makes the higher tones somewhat easier to play.

Formerly the low tones (those written in bass clef) were transposed a fourth below instead of a fifth above. This practice can still be found in scores but the modern practice is also to write the part a fifth higher when it is in bass clef.

(sound)   (old transposition) (modern practice)

Because it has such an extremely long brass tubing, the horn has an extraordinary width of range.

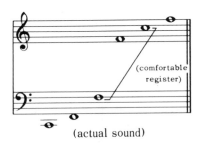

(comfortable register)

(actual sound)

This is somewhat illusory because in actual practice the really fluent and comfortable register is relatively limited.

(written) (sounds)

As the player moves above this comfortable area, the tones rapidly become more and more difficult to produce and consequently very tense and less naturally pleasing.

(written) (sounds)

53

As the player moves down into the notes below, the tones become more and more deep and exotic, and must be thought of as an area for special effect only. The playing in this register requires slower articulation, special preparation and movement that is not too rapid or *staccato*.

(written)   (sounds)

When the horn is "stopped" by inserting the hand, it moves each pitch up a half step from the normal sound. It will not be necessary to make an additional transposition adjustment. The player will transpose these tones mentally and adjust the fingering accordingly. Stopped horn is marked as follows (the European term for this is *bouché*):

(stopped)

The horn tone may be made bland or raucous depending upon the amount of "rattle" or "buzz" that the player imparts to the tone, and the composer can ask for varying degrees of gentleness or vigor by indicating the character of sound desired: e.g., *sotto voce*, "rough," "flexible," etc. The rough brassy sound may be indicated by the term *cuivré*.

Horns can be played flutter-tongue. Trills are possible but should be used with great moderation.

When the horn is muted by inserting the standard mute

into the bell, the tone becomes surprisingly insubstantial. The effect is attractively mysterious and distant.

Originally the horn had no valves and was capable of only a limited use. The modern horn has a much wider capability and need no longer be thought of as a subordinate or background instrument. If given sufficient time between each entrance, the modern horn player is capable of playing almost any reasonably written part. *Legato* demands must allow for sufficient breathing. *Staccato* design must not be too rapid or too long.

Because of the small mouthpiece, the horn is still difficult to play, and consideration should be given to the player's problems of articulation and entry. Since the horn player cannot skip as easily from register to register as other players, the part should be written to move smoothly and consistently within a somewhat limited area.

Hear the famous and challenging horn solo at the beginning of *Till Eulenspiegel* by Strauss. Also listen for the vigorous use of horn in the "Miller's Dance" from *The Three Cornered Hat* by de Falla, the long solo line at the beginning of *Pastorale d'été* by Honegger and the opening horn call in the *Oberon* overture by von Weber.

Study the following examples of typical horn motion.

Andante cantabile

from TCHAIKOVSKY: *Symphony No. 5*

cresc.

from WAGNER: *Siegfried Idyll*

The Trumpet

Italian: *Tromba, Trombe*
French: *Trompette, Trompettes*
German: *Trompete, Trompeten*

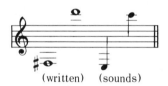

(written)   (sounds)

There are three types of trumpet in general use: (1) the standard orchestral trumpet with its more vigorously strident and martial tone (the archetype of the "clear" brass), (2) the cornet with its mellower tone resulting from the pronounced graduation of the bell and (3) the fluegelhorn, an alto cornet.

The trumpet parts in both band and orchestra will usually be written for B-flat trumpets. The part must be transposed a whole step higher than actual sound. The cornet is pitched exactly the same as the trumpet, and will therefore be in B-flat also and transposed accordingly.

(sounds)   (written)

The fluegelhorn is essentially a deeper and heavier cornet type and is used more in bands than in orchestras. It is usual in the orchestra to use a trumpet for the third part, since this gives a more definitive "clear" brass component to pit against the mellower quality of the horns and trombones. Fluegelhorn would be transposed as a B-flat instrument. Its principal purpose would be to give greater depth to a third part, but it could of course be experimented with melodically.

The practical ranges and registers of the trumpet and cornet are exactly the same.

(written)   (sounds)

Those of the fluegelhorn would be more limited since it specializes in low register.

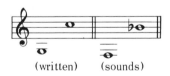

(written)   (sounds)

The few lowest tones of the trumpet are rather inferior in quality and less secure in intonation, and should not be used very often. As the top of the range is approached, the tones become excitingly stringent and furnish an element of intensity well known to composers of dramatic music. Good players like to produce these high tones, but they must be approached somewhat gradually and carefully and the music should not stay very long in this extremely high area because of the effort required.

The trumpets are the loudest of instruments when played *f* or *ff*. This must be taken into consideration when marking the dynamics. When muted they become surprisingly weak.

Traditionally, trumpets have been thought of as instruments of fanfare, and composers of the past too often limited them to a detached articulation. Modern players can do surprisingly well with *legato* effects and should be challenged more often by *legato* melodies and designs. When playing *legato* the player will need to pause for breath, and this should be considered when marking the *legato* phrasing.

Rapid *staccato* is possible but not easy, and should be limited to brief patterns which allow the player time to prepare for each active segment of the pattern.

Twentieth-century developments in the use of mutes have added greatly to the variety of trumpet timbre. For instance, the straight mute creates a silvery, miniaturish sound; the Harmon mute adds a mellower lyricism to the tone; the cup mute produces a genial, slightly mocking distortion. When it had only its natural strident tone, the trumpet was doomed to either foreground or silence. With the invention of the mutes it became possible for the trumpets to play a more subtle role and to contribute a new, more fluid and *legato* action to rhythmic and harmonic background.

For the most striking and modern use of mutes and other trumpet effects, listen with analytical curiosity to all kinds of dance band and jazz recordings. It will also be profitable to observe the remarkable use made by Stravinsky of both open and muted trumpets in *Petrouchka*. In this score there are many instances of trumpet effect which are given the foreground for dramatic purposes. In the Franck *Symphony in D minor* there is unique use of both trumpets and cornets to create a richness of harmonic effect.

Study the following typical trumpet passages.

from BEETHOVEN: *Leonore Overture No. 3*

from WAGNER: *Parsifal*

The Trombone

Italian: *Trombone, Tromboni*
French: *Trombone, Trombones*
German: *Posaune, Posaunen*

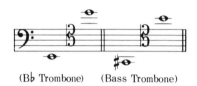

(Bb Trombone)   (Bass Trombone)

The standard trombone is the B-flat or tenor trombone. There is a bass trombone in F that will be found in all the larger professional orchestras. All trombones are nontransposing instruments and the parts are written exactly as they sound.

The natural overtones of the instrument are its most easily played tones. As the slide is extended, lower tones are produced. Below each of the natural overtones a series of half steps will be produced, each half step correlated to one of the seven positions of the slide.

Positions:
1st 2nd 3rd 4th 5th 6th 7th

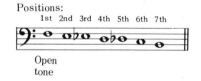

Open
tone

Those tones nearest to the overtone with the least extension of the slide are easiest to play in terms of manipulation of the slide. Rapid motion of the slide from a tone close to the overtone to one the farthest away could create a physical problem, e.g.,

(easy)   (less easy) (difficult)

In slow or gradual extension of the slide there is no problem.

The range and registers of the two trombones are those contained in the illustration below.

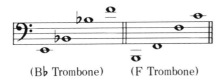

(Bb Trombone)   (F Trombone)

When trombone plays in the high register, the problem of ledger lines makes it customary to write the part in tenor clef.

Since the tone quality of the trombone is somewhere between the "clear" and the "mellow" characteristics of of trumpet and cornet, the composer must "think" it in one or the other of these directions. It can be rich—lyric—noble—ponderous, or vibrant—dynamic—decisive—heroic—strident, depending upon instructions and positive indications by the orchestrator.

Due to the problems connected with the shifting of the

slide, a pure *legato* can be only approximated. Since the articulation or attack is naturally a bit slower than that of trumpet, the trombone *staccato* will be less pointed and biting.

Glissandi are easy in either direction but must be limited to those rather small tonal areas contained within the six half steps below each natural overtone.

Flutter-tongue is possible on trombones.

For effective and varied use of the trombones (and the brasses in general) the symphonies of Tchaikovsky can be recommended. These use powerful lines, declamatory utterances, chordal formations, and rhythmic patterns all intermixed to form great interest and variety in the use of brasses.

The harmonic use of trombones will be discussed in the section on unit organization (page 107).

Study the following typical trombone excerpts.

Maestoso

from RIMSKY-KORSAKOV: *The Russian Easter*

from MCKAY: *Symphonie Miniature No. 2*

The Tuba

Italian: *Tuba*
French: *Tuba*
German: *Basstuba*

The tuba is always written as it sounds. There are several sizes of tuba. The B-flat baritone horn, so called, is really a high-pitched tuba, and in European scores would be called tenor tuba. Other pitches or fundamental tones upon which the tuba's overtone series is founded are C, F, E-flat and low B-flat.

It is the ponderous low B-flat or double B-flat tuba (sometimes called sousaphone) that is used so much in bands and for

63

outdoor music. The higher bass tubas in F and E-flat would have more suitability for orchestral use because of a less ponderous tone and the more available high register values.

Because of the different sizes involved, the composer, more often than not, will indicate tuba on the score and with a certain judicious avoidance of the extremes of high and low register depend upon the player to choose the most suitable tuba type or to play the part on his favorite instrument.

If you specify one of the pitches of tuba, you would then have to be conscious of the following individually different ranges.

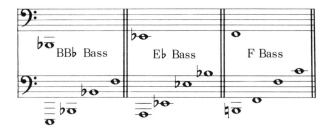

The tuba is most often used as the deep bass tone of the brass choir, but this must not be thought of as a "must." In the orchestra, the bass trombone or the lighter timbre of the third B-flat trombone will be more naturally effective for the third part. The tuba would only be added where phenomenal depth and ponderousness are needed in a third or fourth part or where melody calls for the grotesque interest of one of the extreme tuba registers.

Since the bass tubas are essentially low voice specialists, their lowest registers have a special interest. The typical problems of the tuba are its natural slowness of articulation and attack and a certain sluggishness in *staccato* playing.

On the other hand the tenor tuba, or baritone horn, works out best as an instrument of melody in its characteristically mellow middle and upper registers.

In its role as a supporting bass instrument, keep the tuba well down in the bass area.

In its melodic role, experiment with any reasonably possible upper register, or interestingly deep timbre.

Tubby the Tuba, by Kleinsinger, a children's piece, illustrates tuba potentialities.

PERCUSSION INSTRUMENTS (with indefinite pitch)

To write for the percussion instruments with indefinite pitches, the orchestrator must choose between three methods of indication:

(1) on the third space of a separate staff in bass clef

(2) on a separate staff in treble clef

(3) on a single line without clef

Any of these three will suffice, although it might be argued that the treble clef is correct for high sounds and the bass for low sounds. It might also be argued that the single line makes more sense than either of the clefs, since it both singles out the percussion and saves space on the printed score.

Before writing any percussion into the score, think seriously about its purpose. Percussion is so vivid that its excitement and impact must not be wasted in random use. Percussion is best used (1) as a punctuation or definition for attack and climax, (2) for vivid rhythmic effect, (3) for dramatic characterization, (4) as a means for building *crescendi*, (5) for subtle tone mixing, (6) to create orchestral design through interesting patterns pitted against patterns in other sections.

Think out your purpose and apply just the right timbre and rhythmic pattern.

Although they are immediately exciting when they first enter, the idiophonic (percussive) instruments become somewhat wearing if overused. Like seasoning, they must be used sparingly and in just the right amount. When they enter briefly for sudden emphasis or punctuation, there is a keenness of impact and a sense of happy surprise. The rhythmic excitement of percussion adds a mysterious substance and glamor to orchestration, but only when the percussive timbres chosen have a fitness for the music being played. Avoid routine use of the noisy military instruments and experiment with the more subtle and delicate percussive sounds.

Some percussion instruments, like the snare drum, bass drum, and cymbals, are naturally loud, and must be given dynamic markings that will moderate their intensity.

However, certain other exotic percussion sounds are extremely delicate. Be on the alert about dynamic problems whenever you write for percussion.

The following chart gives a résumé of the generalities of percussion motion.

Percussion Effects

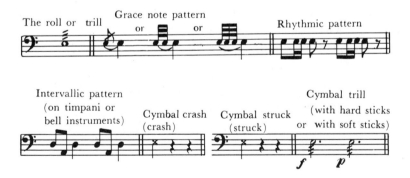

67

Drums

Among the many drums of indefinite pitch, the snare drum and the bass drum have long dominated the musical scene. In basic timbre they are really less interesting than some of the more exotic drums, the tabla (from India), the tabor (from old England), the tom-tom and the numerous African drum types. Drums can be struck with the hands or with either hard or soft sticks.

Perhaps its versatility has caused the long life and popularity of the snare drum. It can be played muted by muffling with a cloth, the clattering wooden edge can be brought into play either by a sudden stroke (rim shot) or by a more elaborate and entertainingly brittle design.

(wooden side of drum)

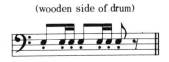

It can be played without the snare and when played with the snare vibrating it can bring in a great variety of vigorously active design. The fundamentals of snare drum pattern are categorized in the following example.

(flam)   (ruff)   (ratamacue)   (paradiddle)   (roll)

Snare drum adds much to *crescendi* and to moments of punctuation but it should not be used except where it is valid to some dynamic or dramatic purpose.

The bass drum is roundly resonant and can be quite loud. It responds rather slowly and is therefore suited to relatively simple and well spaced patterns. Indicate either hard or soft stick. Be conscious of whether you want it to resound or be played dryly (as *staccato* as possible). Indicate exactly the quality you want the player to try for.

Search through your community to discover any existing drums of the more exotic type and bring them into the classroom for experimental study.

Cymbals

Italian: *Piatti*
French: *Cymbales*
German: *Becken*

The orchestral cymbals can be played either by being crashed together (the cymbal crash), or struck by either hard or soft stick. The cymbal may be struck repeatedly and gently to cause a rhythmic pattern or struck strongly and allowed to ring. The symbol for the crash is as follows.

(crash)

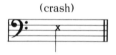

When the cymbal is to be struck, use the word (struck) in parentheses and write out the rhythms to be produced.

(struck-hard stick)   (struck-soft stick)

A special type of sound related to the cymbal is the tam-tam (not to be confused with the tom-tom) or gong. When struck loudly the effect is startling and dramatic. When struck softly there is a poetic lingering quality. It is so shatteringly different in sound that one use is about enough in any one composition.

The Tambourine

Italian: *Tamburino* (or *Tamburo basco*)
French: *Tambour de Basque*
German: *Schellentrommel* (or *Tambourin*)

The tambourine is really a small drum type, but the jingles or brass discs around the edge give it its unique timbre. It can be shaken

(shaken)

or struck

(struck)

or it can give an illusion of the trill by rubbing with the thumb.

(thumb trill)

The Wood Block

The wood block is another exotic departure from the drum prototype and gives an entertainingly dry, brittle and rather comic sound when struck by either snare drum sticks or xylophone sticks (specify which stick to use in striking the wood block).

Castanets

Italian: *Castagnette*
French: *Castagnettes*
German: *Kastagnetten*

Castanets are hollowed-out shells of hard wood which are held two in each hand for playing. They can either click out fundamental rhythms

or they can simulate the trill.

The Triangle

Italian: *Triangolo*
French: *Triangle*
German: *Triangel*

The triangle can also create a rhythm or simulate the trill. It is wise to limit the triangle to single bits of luminous reinforcement. An overuse tends to make it commonplace or too literal. When the triangle came in with a trill in the wrong place during a rehearsal, Sir Thomas Beecham is said to have remarked, "Will someone kindly answer the telephone."

PERCUSSION INSTRUMENTS (with definite pitch)

The Timpani

Italian: *Timpani*
French: *Timbales*
German: *Pauken*

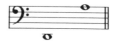

There are four sizes of timpani, or "kettledrums," each with a limited range.

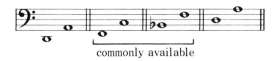

commonly available

Most orchestral writing will be limited to the practical range of one octave.

Amateur and school orchestras will usually have only two drums, but the larger professional orchestras will have all of them.

The timbre differences can be sensed, ranging from a certain thunderous dryness of the very lowest drum (the least-often used) to the warmer tenor resonance of the highest drum.

A single player will usually play all of the drums used and he must be given time to tune them if the pitches are to be other than those to which they have been tuned at the beginning.

Let us suppose that two drums are being used.

73

One drum will be tuned to sound A,

another drum will be tuned to sound D.

Drums can be sounded together (but this is rarely done).

By playing the two drums at the pitches to which they have been set in advance, a great variety of patterns is available.

Each of the drums can be changed at any time to a new pitch contained within its range (see Example 90), but the player must be given definite instructions in his part. "Change from A to B," for instance. The important thing to remember is that with the hand-tuned timpani the player must have ample time to make the change by tuning, and that if a drastic change to a higher or lower pitch is called for, even more time will be necessary.

Where the player is using the recently invented "pedal timpani," the tuning is done quickly and easily by a foot pedal. Pitch changes must be specified but a much greater variety of tones is available because of the relative ease of change.

A soft stick is almost always used, and by alternating two sticks rapidly on one drum, a trill or "roll" is effected.

Timpani, because of relatively uninteresting uniformity of timbre, need the compensating value of interesting dynamics.

Not only do the dynamics need to be interesting enough, they also need to be most carefully calculated, since the timpani can be quickly destructive to the dynamic balance when played too loudly.

Each drum of the pedal type can be played *glissando*, an upward or downward slide effected by pushing down or lifting the pedal, but the tones must be limited to the narrow range of a single drum.

75

The Glockenspiel

(written)   (sounds)

Italian: *Campanelli*
French: *Jeu de timbres* (or *Carillon*)
German: *Glockenspiel*

The metal bars of the glockenspiel, arranged to simulate a piano keyboard, have a series of half steps sounding two octaves above the following range.

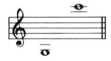

Write the notes within the range as given above.

Normally the player will play a single melodic line that does not move too rapidly. By holding more than one stick in either hand he can play a few well-chosen supplementary chords.

The sound is sweetly bell-like but, because of the lingering resonance of tones previously struck, the sound tends to blur when the glockenspiel is played too rapidly.

All bell sounds become tiresome rather quickly and the glockenspiel is typical in this tendency to become cloying to the ear. Used in moderation it can add a special poetic quality.

The Xylophone

Italian: *Silofono* (or *Xilofono*)
French: *Xylophone*
German: *Xylophon*

Like the glockenspiel, the xylophone also has a chromatic scale arranged like the keys of the piano keyboard. The comfortable range is within these notes.

Larger xylophones include a few notes higher and lower.

The dry, brittle and woody tone allows a faster motion than the glockenspiel, and the xylophone prospers when used with a certain amount of virtuosity. It also is very effective for punctuation, tone mixing and for bell simulation. There is a certain raucous, comic side to its sound that is useful in characterization.

77

The Marimba

The marimba is like a xylophone with resonating chambers. Its range is

(actual sounds)

The Vibraphone

The vibraphone is like a glockenspiel with resonating chambers. Its range is

The Tubular Bells (or Chimes)

Italian: *Campane*
French: *Cloches*
German: *Glocken*

The tubular bells or "chimes" are used occasionally. The effect is rather literal since it is so much associated with liturgical suggestion, and the tone is loud and positive in timbre. Restraint and sparing use are suggested.

The Celesta

Italian: *Celesta*
French: *Celesta*
German: *Celesta*

The celesta is a piano keyboard with a luscious "celestial" bell sound. See the chart on page 6 for the range. It can articulate tones rather rapidly but does need a bit of time in which to resound.

MISCELLANEOUS SOUND EFFECTS

Various noise makers have been employed in music from time to time, automobile horns, whistles, rattles, sleigh bells, the whip, etc. The popular audience loves this sort of realism but the artistic limits are quickly reached. Search out and employ anything of this sort that is available in your community for experiment. Specify the particular noise maker in the score— e.g., "automobile chains" (shake)—and then indicate the rhythm on a staff or line.

Numerous exotic instruments may also be mentioned, such as maracas, Indian rattles, bongos, etc., etc. Much exploration needs to be done. Search out some sophisticated drummer in your community and invite him into the class for experiments with any exotic instruments available.

THE PIANO

In the high register of the piano there are marvelous potentialities for bell-like chordal complexities that no other instrument can equal. In the middle register there are resources for a fluency of motion that can add subtle elaboration to accompanimental

79

background (Manuel de Falla has made much of this possibility in *El Amor Brujo*). In the low register there are extraordinary *marcato* percussive intensities useful for punctuating and thickening the bass sounds. When the piano is used routinely or for ordinary doubling, the result is dull. If used in the orchestra it should have its own independent and imaginative part.

Works which show a particularly inventive and effective use of the piano as an orchestral instrument are *El Amor Brujo* by de Falla and *Petrouchka* by Stravinsky.

PLECTRUM INSTRUMENTS

The modern re-emergence of the plucked or plectrum instruments has brought back a basic orchestral ingredient. *Pizzicato* string tone has been present but it is less vivid than the plectrum effect of harpsichord, harp and guitar.

The Harpsichord

The delicious "jangle" of the harpsichord is very valuable as an orchestral ingredient. Its unique plectrum articulation is more vivid than that of the harp, and it furnishes a *staccato* intensity that is strikingly resonant and continuous.

The harpsichord is essentially an instrument of motion, but it can also make a striking orchestral effect by sudden chordal punctuations. Its timbre is so resonantly typical of plectrum sound that it combines wonderfully with almost any other timbre and especially well with strings or woodwinds. To hear harpsichord in its orchestral relation, listen to the *Harpsichord Concerto* by de Falla and *Petite Symphonie Concertante* by Martin.

The harpsichord range is encompassed within the following limits:

The Harp

The harp has the following range:

The harp furnishes excitement and motion principally by means of the *glissando*. To create this effect the hands sweep freely over the strings. Before this is done the strings must be set into the desired tonal pattern by shifting the pedals.

Once the strings are set, the harpist is free to create any rapid or unusual *glissando* pattern. It is necessary to indicate the tones desired for each of the letter names of the scale. C can be pitched at C-natural, C-sharp or C-flat; D can be pitched at D-natural, D-sharp or D-flat, etc. These must be indicated at the beginning of the *glissando*. Any up or down motion should be indicated by a line (see page 82).

Before any new tones can be introduced, the foot pedals

must be shifted, and the player must be given sufficient time to make this adjustment.

A variety of delicate patterns are possible through the use of the *staccato* or plectrum sound made by plucking the strings. Harmonics are effected by stopping the string lightly at a point one-half or one-quarter of the distance up its length. When harmonics are to be played, the player must be given time to prepare for each tone.

For orchestral purposes the harp is essentially an instrument of motion. Too much harmonic emphasis in the part can slow up action. The most imaginative writing should almost always feature either relatively elaborate *glissando* motion or rather simple, pointed and direct *staccato* motion.

The harp tone is weak and easily obliterated except when set in motion by vigorous *glissando* playing.

To hear the harp in action as an orchestral ingredient, such scores by Debussy as *La Mer, Ibéria* and *Danses sacrée et profane* are outstanding. The *Harp Concerto* by Glière, available as a recording (as are most of the works mentioned in this book), will illustrate effective and typical writing for the harp as used in solo work with orchestra.

Harp Effects

Glissando (tones to be included indicated at beginning)

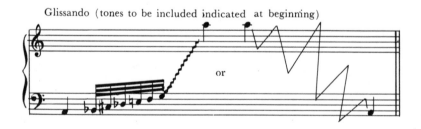

or

Harp Effects

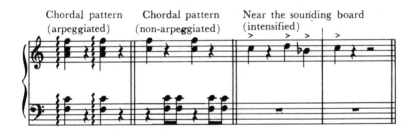

The Guitar

The guitar has begun to be a more and more important part of music generally and can be heard in an orchestral relation in *Concierto de Aranjuez* by Rodrigo.

83

The guitar has the following strings:

The guitar plays melody, chords and some arpeggiated figures. Chords and arpeggiated design must be accommodated to the finger position required. Practical combinations can be found and impossibilities avoided by calculating fingerings that will be natural to the hand, with needed tones chosen to make use of the natural string order.

The classic guitar has nylon strings as opposed to the more popular metal strings. The nylon-stringed guitar has a corresponding delicacy of tone that must be either accommodated for in scoring or aided by a microphone.

STRING INSTRUMENTS

The strings have many uses and values and have long been the fundamental timbre of the orchestra. They have a superior pliability and a greater variety of effect than the other families of instruments. This results from the great range of articulatory possibility that can be had from the bow, and the striking contrast between the *pizzicato* (plucked) and *arco* (bowed) sounds.

Rules For Bowing and Phrasing

If written with only the usual slurs and dots to indicate *legato* and *staccato*, the strings will always be played with the bow. To indicate the use of *pizzicato* or plucked tone, write *pizz.* above the staff at the point at which this effect is to begin.

To cancel the plucked articulation and return to bowed sound, write the word *arco* above the point at which the return to bowed sound is desired.

When the bow is being used, all notes included in one slur will be played on a single bow, either up- or down-bow.

Unless otherwise marked, the first slur in each measure will automatically be played with a down-bow.

Down-bow is marked with this sign:

⊓

Up-bow is marked with this sign:

V

In general, there will be two bows to a measure with down-bow and up-bow alternating.

There are, however, endless exceptions to this, depending upon the character and dynamics of the music. When playing softly, the string player can often use a single bow to the measure, but in *forte* playing he will need more bows.

If down-bow and up-bow alternate continuously this is the most natural pattern and does not need to be marked.

All notes included under a single slur will be played by one bow.

If a phrase begins with an up-beat or *anacrusis* it is understood without marking that it will be played up-bow. If down-bow is preferred it must be indicated.

Any desired deviation from the regular alternation of down-bow and up-bow must be marked accordingly.

Successive down-bows give a powerful hammered effect.

86

Successive up-bows are more light and graceful.

Separated notes with dots indicate varied types of *staccato* which must be defined for the player by further description in Italian: *spiccato, saltato, martele;* or by the English meaning: "rapidly and lightly," "jumping bow," "hammered," etc.

Separate notes with dots may be included in a slur, with the type of dot indicating intensity of articulation.

Whenever dots are used under a slur to indicate successive down-bows or successive up-bows, or whenever any deviation from the normal alternation is brought into the phrasing, mark indications for the bowing which will return it as soon as possible to the normal alternation (down-bow, up-bow).

It is sometimes effective to have accented points in a phrase at the end of a bow, but this is a special effect and an exception.

Intervals and Chords

String instruments can sometimes play two notes at once, either plucked or bowed, if tones are chosen carefully. Two tones sounding together on the same instrument are known as "double stops." Since the strings are arranged to sound a series of open fifths when no fingers are used, these "open strings" are the key to the choice of intervals to be used in double stopping.

Violin strings   Viola strings Cello strings   Bass strings

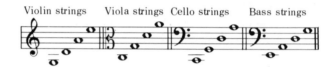

All fifths and sixths are relatively easy for the fingers. Because two strings can be covered by the same finger, consecutive perfect fifths can be played easily and rapidly.

(easy)   (relatively easy)

All fourths, thirds, seconds and augmented fourths are relatively difficult, but if the upper tone is an open string any of these is very easy to play.

(relatively difficult)   (easy)

Octaves and sevenths which have an open string as the lower tone are very easy to play, and because of the comfortable position of the hand are not too difficult even without the open string.

However, double stops, except for the consecutive fifths, must usually be articulated with separate bows, or plucked, and ample time must be given the player to adjust the hand to a series of differing double stops.

Three-tone chords can be played if strongly stroked with the bow or strummed for *pizzicato* effect, but the tones must be carefully chosen to include intervals and hand positions that are practicable. Any combination of superimposed sixths, or fifths and sixths, works out easily.

(relatively easy)   (easy)   (relatively easy)

Since two tones cannot be played at once on the same string, be sure that three different strings are being used. If one or two of the strings are open the chords will usually be very resonant and easy to play.

(easy)

Because of the general fogginess of the lower pitches, double stops do not prosper on the cello and bass. If double stops or chords are written for either bass or cello, it is best to include as much open string sound as possible as an aid to clarity.

Cello

Note that while the strings of violin, viola and cello are arranged in fifths, those of the bass are arranged in fourths, and any calculation of double stop and chord possibilities will have to accommodate to these open strings.

Harmonics

The string instruments have two kinds of harmonics, natural and artificial. The natural harmonic is produced by touching the string lightly at points which are found either one quarter, one half or one third the length of the string, and then drawing the bow. They are marked as follows:

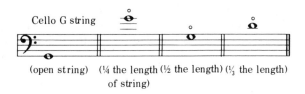

Cello G string

(open string)　(¼ the length　(½ the length) (⅓ the length)
of string)

Artificial harmonics are produced by putting one finger down firmly and another down lightly at distances of either a fourth or fifth above. The placing of the finger a fourth above produces a tone two octaves higher.

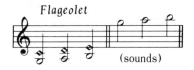

Flageolet

(sounds)

When placed a fifth above, the tone is an octave and a fifth higher.

Flageolet

(sounds)

The natural harmonics are very secure tones and can be used as sustaining effect. The artificial harmonics are less secure and must be used with sufficient preparation and with delicacy of background.

All of the strings have these harmonics, and the lower the string, the more substantial the harmonics are (cello and bass).

The following examples will show all the principal string effects and their typical markings.

String Effects

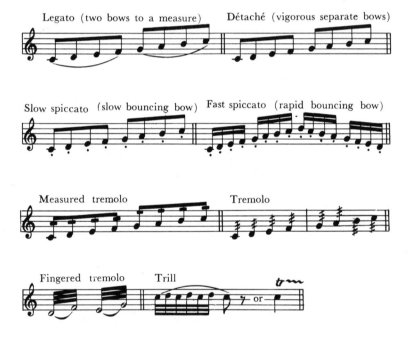

String Effects

String Effects

Natural harmonics on the D string (each
open string has harmonics in the same ratio)

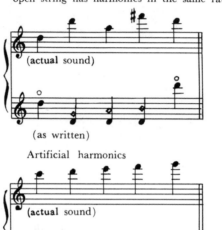

(actual sound)

(as written)

Artificial harmonics

(actual sound)

(as written)

Col legno (drum with the back of the bow) Pizzicato (plucked)

pizz.

Ponticello (bow very near
the bridge and slanted toward   Sul tasto or flautando (soft bowing away
player)   from bridge – forward on the fingerboard)

Non-vibrato   Divisi
(non-vibrato)   Div.

94

The Violin

Italian: *Violino, Violini*
French: *Violon, Violons*
German: *Violine, Violinen*

The range of the violin is uniformly effective. See chart of registers (page 5).

There are a few tones above the highest G that will sometimes be found and of these the A and B are very clear and usable. Above these the tones are seldom used.

The tone quality is clear and even throughout the violin range. Each of the four strings has some timbre difference but it is the high tones of the E string (bright and clear) and the low tones of the G string (warm and deep) that will be singled out most often. The A and D strings are beautifully eloquent.

Each of the strings is sometimes featured separately for its special timbre. The markings for this are *Sul G, Sul D* and *Sul A*. Instead of moving to the tones of the string immediately above, the player plays higher on the one string.

Sul G (on the G string)

BACH-WILHELMJ

95

Although the violin has long been the principal voice of the orchestra, do not overlook its modern role of supplying background. It is wonderfully suited to this in its neutral registers. The string tone has a special pliability and a potentiality for softness and gentleness that makes it particularly suited for use as general background. The woodwinds, brass and percussion have a more insistent vividness and force of impact. Because of this difference in tonal character, the ear can tolerate the string tone for longer periods of continuous use.

When writing for the violin, give the player time to make the change from *pizzicato* to bowed sound, or vice versa. In *legato* passages two bows per measure are generally required to ensure that the player will have enough bow for a full, free tone. Be reasonable in asking for rapid and continuous leaps from high to low register (across the strings). Be inventive enough with the bowing (mixing *staccato* and *legato*) to avoid a monotony of articulation.

If too much rapidity is not expected, the violin, in common with all the rest of the strings, can make leaps from register to register with considerable ease.

(easy)   (easy)   (difficult)

All trills are possible, but tremolos larger than a fourth must be generally avoided as these must be accomplished by fingering on a single string.

The range of articulatory differences is large—from a mere whisper to the savage hammering effect of successive down-bows played *ff*.

Violins, especially, prosper when phrased imaginatively

and vividly. Fundamentally, this will demand a positive inter-action between *staccato* and *legato* and between uneven and even accenting (see Project 32, page 251).

To see subtle and interesting phrasing and marking of string parts, study the string quartets of Haydn, Mozart and Beethoven, and those of Debussy, Ravel and Bartók. Also, listen to the recordings of the principal violin concertos played by the best violinists to get an idea of the sound of the violin in its typical registers and the relation of *staccato* and *legato* to its idiomatic effectiveness.

The Viola

The viola has the range given below.

It is always written in the alto clef except for the few highest tones, which may be written in treble clef if the alto clef ledger lines become a problem.

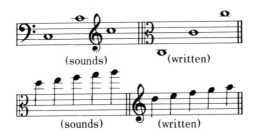

(sounds)   (written)

(sounds)   (written)

97

This mellow alto instrument has all the versatility of the violin, but it responds a little less quickly to demands for motion and is more subdued in tone. You cannot expect power from the violas, but you can expect a highly attractive melodic character and much usefulness in accompanimental design. The lower and higher registers are most unusual because of the gruff, slightly hoarse, charm of the C-string, and the poignant and nasal, but poetically expressive, timbre of the high A-string.

The *Suite* for viola and piano by Bloch reaches deeply and originally into viola effect—hear it.

The Cello

Italian: *Violoncello, Violoncelli*
French: *Violoncelle, Violoncelles*
German: *Violoncell, Violoncelle*

The comfortable register of the cello extends from a low C

up to high A.

98

In its upper register it is written in tenor clef.

The few highest tones from A to E are written in treble clef, but intonation is risky and these tones are not often used.

There are certain natural limitations to the possibilities of the cello. It can play rapidly, but not as easily as the violin and viola. It can play chords, but in the orchestra they tend to blur. The cello has an especially good melodic register on the A-string. The first octave of this A-string register is easy to play and is expressively eloquent. Higher up, extreme intonation difficulties begin.

It is possible for the cellist to do all types of bowing and produce all the trills, *tremolos* and harmonics that the violinist and violist are able to, but he needs just a little more time to prepare for the problems peculiar to cello playing. The composer must take into consideration the need for heavier finger pressure on the thicker cello strings, the slower action of the shorter, heavier bow, and the larger distances required of the hand in shifting position.

The middle register of the cello is neither vivid for melodic use nor effective as bass line. A bass line will usually employ the lower tones, while typical cello melody will tend to exploit the upper register.

99

For listening experiences in effective cello writing, hear the concertos by Saint-Saëns and Schumann and *Schelomo* by Bloch.

The Double Bass

Italian: *Contrabasso, Contrabassi*
French: *Contrebasse, Contrebasses*
German: *Kontrabass, Kontrabasse*

(written)   (sounds)

The double bass is a transposing instrument. It must be written an octave higher than it sounds.

When the bass is used as a solo instrument, its plaintive and somewhat grotesque upper register is featured.

When doubling the cello an octave lower (its ordinary supporting role) it is best to use middle register. The lower tones tend to be a bit dry, gruff and heavy. The upper tones do not give the true bass effect.

The resonance of the bass section is very powerful and can well be played *pizzicato* a good part of the time.

Do not always double the cello part exactly. Sometimes the technical difficulties of the cello part (rapid runs and elaborate design) will be beyond the possibilities of the slower-moving double bass and not natural to its idiomatic quality. When the cello is very elaborate, double only the principal tones in an approximation of the cello design.

from BEETHOVEN: *Symphony No. 7*

Since the bass bow is relatively short, detached bowing will be more natural for most passages. The amount of *legato* should be moderate.

INSTRUMENTAL MOTION

Do not take the supposed incapabilities of players and instruments *too* seriously. Challenge players with stimulating musical designs. All instruments have idiomatic possibilities which can be set in motion to produce a kind of kinesthetic excitement which is the very essence or orchestral interest. All players respond with enthusiasm when given something to do within the orchestral fabric that brings out their feeling of creative contribution to the result. Avoid "dead" or "routine" motion.

Although effective motion is a principal means of orchestration, the need is not so much for mere "liveliness" as for effective and interesting design. Simplicity and repose are also virtues.

Although the structural glamor and originality of the outstanding composers' orchestration seem to result from sheer genius in exuberant motor invention, these individualized motion patterns will nearly always stem from certain fundamental types of motion. These are illustrated below in skeletonized form.

101

Types of Instrumental Motion

(a) the trill:

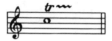

(b) the *tremolo*:

(c) reiterated *staccato*:

(d) *staccato* arpeggiation:

(e) *legato* arpeggiation:

(f) the run:

(g) wave pattern:

(staccato)   (legato)

(h) reiterated rhythmic pattern:

(i) leaps:

(j) alternation of entrance:

(k) alternation of *staccato* and *legato*:

(l) expansion:

(Strings)

A trill harmonically expanded

(m) development:

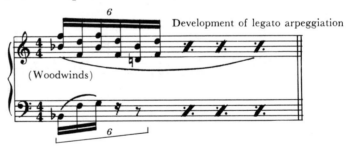

Development of legato arpeggiation

(Woodwinds)

(n) combination:

Combination of the run, repeated rhythmic pattern, and alternation of entrance

Study scores and recordings to observe how these basic types have been caused to flower out into originality of design.

Scores and recordings of works especially written to illustrate the various instruments will be valuable for this. Listen to *The Young Person's Guide to the Orchestra* by Benjamin Britten and Bartók's *Concerto for Orchestra*, a work in which each instrument is featured soloistically at some point.

Fully developed knowledge of orchestral techniques requires much experience. Study various orchestral scores to see how the elements of design have been transformed into new and original patterns. Take advantage of every possible opportunity to hear orchestral music in rehearsal. Analyze the relation of instrumental motion to listening experience, and whenever possible discuss, with players, orchestral parts you have written for them. To know, experience; to learn, do.

2

Principles of Clarity

INTENTIONAL CONFUSION OR VAGUENESS CAN SOMETIMES contribute to dramatic interest, but orchestration is usually the most effective when it is clear or definite. Conversely, it is not effective when the result is confused or vague. Clarity in orchestration results from positive (definite) organization of sounds and structures by means of certain types of control. Each of these types of control will be explained and illustrated. Following each explanation a study project will be outlined, to be used as a guide to experimentation.

The exercises written for completion of these projects need not be long. A few measures will suffice to try out each principle. The object is to do many exercises in order to achieve experimentation over the total range of basic technique.

Write most exercises in actual sound, in reduced score—with the woodwinds at the top, brass next to the top and percussion and strings placed at the bottom (woodwinds, brass, percussion, strings).

After you have written and heard your own example, search through the works of some of the master composers—particularly such recent composers as Bartók, Stravinsky, Hindemith and Prokofiev—to see how they have applied the same technique.

It is hoped that students will create original music for use in these projects. It will be more of an adventure to write and hear your own composition—even the simplest of diatonic harmonies will suffice for testing out the various techniques.

However, for those with less experience a workbook has been provided, with convenient musical excerpts to be used in fulfilling the projects by arranging. The workbook also contains blank pages of music score.

CONSISTENCY OF UNIT ORGANIZATION

The ear naturally tends to separate the different families of sound into units of tonal action and to focus similar timbres into unified meaning.

Because of this tendency, achievement of clarity demands that instruments of similar timbre (woodwinds, brass, strings, and percussion) be grouped into units that are rhythmically and harmonically consistent.

There are no immutable laws governing this grouping, since matters of preference will always enter into the writing of any music. However, certain general suggestions can be offered.

(1) Groups usually consist of instruments of related or similar timbre: e.g., four horns, four strings, three woodwinds, etc.

(2) Each group should be rhythmically consistent and harmonically complete, and should make musical sense when played separately.

(3) Groups may be made up of any number of voices, but two-, three-, and four-voice units are the most common. A single line may be used as a representative grouping, since it is obviously consistent in design.

(4) Harmonically full groupings of more than four voices are quite often used, but it should be remembered that rich-sounding chords tend to obliterate clarity of design. If one group has many harmonic voices, other groups sounding at

the same time should ordinarily counter this by using few voices.

(5) The harmonic spacing of a group can be open or close, depending upon preference, but once a spacing has been established it should, as a rule, continue.

(too sudden except for grotesque effect)

(6) All groups should ordinarily use the same general harmonic progression, but each can have its own independent disposition of parts. If each group is harmonically complete in its own right there is no further harmonic organization needed.

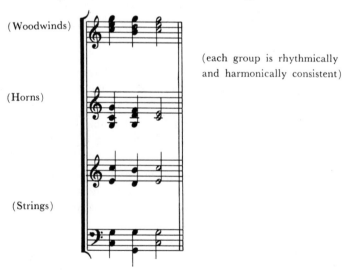

(each group is rhythmically and harmonically consistent)

(7) Different groups sounding simultaneously may have different rhythms or similar rhythms, but the rhythmic relationship of two or more groups should be inclined toward either contrast or similarity.

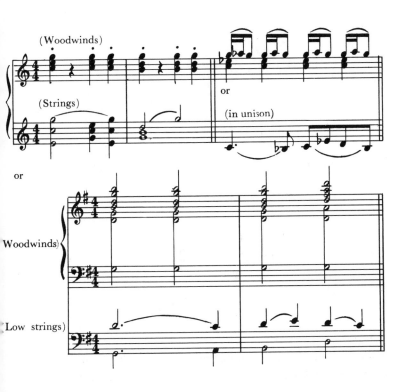

(8) Dissonant or clashing melodic and decorative tones are softened and absorbed when groups of contrasting timbre are sounded simultaneously (see the example on page 237).

Types of Harmonic Distribution

Before going on to the special preparatory assignments of Project 1 (consistency of unit organization), it will be necessary to understand normal harmonic distributions typical of the different families of timbre.

An ordinary group of two will usually be within the same timbre.

Oboes 1-2 Horns 1-2

Woodwinds in two-part units tend to be distributed as follows:

A group of three will be either two of one timbre combined with a different timbre of the same family or three of a kind.

Two different distributions of woodwinds in three-voice units are shown below.

Four-part groupings are either superimposed,

overlapped (intermixed)

or enclosed.

Normal distribution of the full brass group is shown below.

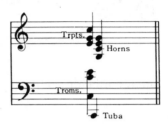

String distribution is more free than that of woodwinds and brasses, but the usual spacing is open harmony as in the following:

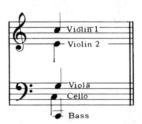

This next example illustrates the fuller sound that results from strengthening the center and doubling the upper melody an octave higher.

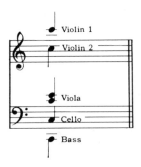

The following illustrates a typical *divisi* distribution:

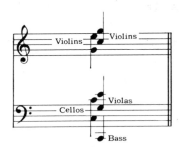

Project 1

Project 1 will consist of special assignments in harmonic distribution. For illustration, the same harmonization will be shown distributed in nine different ways: three in woodwind, three in brass and three in strings. After studying these harmonic distributions, the student will either search out a suitable harmonic subject, compose an original one or use the one given in the workbook. By using the illustrations as models he will then complete the preparatory assignments that follow.

Harmonic Subject

from GRIEG: *Op. 68, No. 1*

All examples for assignments (a) through (i) are in actual sound.

(a) A three-voice woodwind unit:

GRIEG

Use the above distribution of three voices as a model for harmonization.

Use this same excerpt for all the remaining assignments.

(b) Two-voice woodwind units combined:

Change of key offers better registers.

Play each two-part group separately (and note that it makes structural sense by itself).

In choosing a successful key, let outer voice register needs determine choice.

Imitate the above model.

(c) Three-voice woodwind units combined:

Play each group of three separately to sense its harmonic completeness.

Both melody and bass are doubled in octaves to balance overall harmonic fullness.

In a group this full, all instruments do not have to play all the time.

Imitate the above model.

(d) Brass in two-voice units:

2 Trpts.

2 Horns

Imitate the above model.

(e) The complete brass choir:

Trumpets and trombones work together.
Horns are in a thinner contrasting texture.

Imitate the above model.

(f) Expanded brass choir:

Tuba register governed this choice of keys.
Brasses are good in flat keys.

Imitate the above model.

(g) Standard open harmony in strings:

Strings are **natural** to sharp keys.

(h) Reinforced open harmony:

Register for doubled melody governed choice of key; also brings into play a suitably deep bass register.

(i) Multiple strings—*divisi*:

Try for effective register, interesting design.

Prepare examples of string distribution based on the above models.

As you do these assignments in harmonic distribution, keep in mind that they do not represent authoritative or required distributions to be used in all future writing. They are only

123

meant for first acquaintance with the problems of harmonic distribution and as general exercises.

After you understand the general principles and have done these preparatory assignments, you should engage in constant exploratory experimentation. Try all sorts of unusual groupings and spacings, place instruments out of their normal order (bassoons above clarinets, oboes above flutes, etc., etc.) in search of sounds of unusual interest. Mix open and close harmony in various unusual ways.

Also remember that, in actual practice, smaller, thinner groupings are used much more than the more luscious fuller groupings and that you must constantly be on the alert to keep the lower registers from being too heavy in sound or too muddy. But even here, experimentation is in order. Find out exactly how to make these harmonies in the low register most effective. Bruckner uses a choir of tubas in one of his symphonies. Berlioz uses a group of four timpani playing chords in the *Symphonie Fantastique*. It *can* be done, if the extreme low harmonies are clearly isolated.

Write all of these assignments in actual sound. If they are to be tried out in performance, the transposing instruments will need transposed parts. Refer to the chart of transposition ratios on page 7).

DEFINITENESS OF TEXTURE

There are certain elementary types of unity which are necessary for clarity of musical meaning. These will be referred to as *textures*. They are types of "togetherness" in musical action, and are particularly necessary to orchestral writing because of the many diverse sounds and motor potentialities which, if left unorganized, would incline toward confusion. Any musical ensemble will profit from clear and definite design (positive texture).

There are eight fundamental texture types:

(a) *monophonic* texture:

(concentration of action into a single reinforced line)

(b) *chordal* texture:

(concentration into vertical blocks of sound)

(c) *polyphonic* texture:

(unity through line similarity)

(d) *homophonic* texture:

(unity through contrast of role)

(e) *polythematic* texture:

(unity through contrast of motive)

(f) *polyrhythmic* texture:

(unity through blended rhythmic action)

(g) *heterophonic* texture:

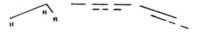

(unity of theme and variation played simultaneously)

(h) *onomatopoeic* texture:

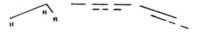

(thunder)   (lightning)

(unity through nature imitation)

The application of the word "texture" to music may need to be defended. The main definition as given in the dictionary is: "texture—the peculiar disposition of the constituent parts of any body; the manner in which they are disposed, arranged or united; structure in general." Surely this definition includes music (a body of sound).

Each of these textural types will be fully explained and illustrated and study projects suggested. After the several textural projects have been completed, it should be clear that every score must necessarily utilize one or another of the textures at any point in its progress, since they are indispensable sources of unity.

Monophonic Texture

Of the eight types of texture, the simplest is the *monophonic*. Monophonic means "single-voiced" or "unisonal," but in the orchestra such unison can be composed of either a single line or any amount of octave doubling.

One use of monophonic texture is in the so-called "grand unison," with all instruments doubling in their natural registers (see preceding example); or the instruments may be used to produce an intense and concentrated single line in middle register (such as viola, cello, horn, high bassoon, or low clarinet).

127

The instruments may be widely spaced for unusual effect.

The doubling may include register and timbre variegation.

There may be differentiated articulation.

Variegation of pitch locale and articulation, and a certain effect of light and shade achieved by alternating octave doubling with single line, all contribute to a needed variety. If the experimental procedure also includes variegation of timbre, it can be seen that the possibilities for monophonic interest are far-reaching indeed.

The creative and historical importance of the monophonic texture is evidenced by the emphasis that it received in early European and Oriental music. A study of the music of India and China gives a vision of the possibilities to be explored. The student is referred to the Louisville Symphony recording *And The Fallen Petals* by Chou Wen-Chung. This is an outstanding example of essentially monophonic procedure, intensely variegated with much variety of timbre and much use of percussion.

Project 2

Write short monophonic examples as suggested in the workbook. The unison line will furnish such a tight and intense unity that the music will be monotonous unless enough variety is brought in as a counteracting force. Make full use of variety of register and timbre. Use some percussion to intensify the effect, and alternate between octave doubling and unison line.

The musical power of unisonal music is sometimes astoundingly effective and must not be underrated. The expressive poignance of Gregorian chant is an illustration of the values of the monophonic texture.

Experiment with the rapid change of timbre within a continuing line (the Webern concept of "Klang Farben" concentratedly applied). Also experiment with dramatically vivid unisonal mixtures with expressive vigor in mind (qualities of comedy, ruggedness, languor etc.).

from RIMSKY-KORSAKOV: *Scheherazade* (Eulenberg)

PLATE I. MONOPHONIC TEXTURE

Chordal Texture

Chordal texture is the opposite of monophonic texture. Monophonic texture results from a concentrated horizontal emphasis. Chordal texture results from a concentrated vertical emphasis. The unity of the monophonic texture is a focus of musical action into line. The unity of the chordal texture is a focus of musical action into blocks of sound. These blocks of sound have two continuing characteristics: (1) harmonic impact, and (2) similar rhythm in the several voices. Note these characteristics in the example below:

This miraculously simple theme, from Beethoven's *Symphony No. 7*, has a certain restricted and hymn-like motion that is natural to the chordal texture. However, chordal texture has other more active possibilities and most of these will come into action because of the need of the extremely compact unity of the chordal texture to be balanced by variety. This variety can be supplied by the rhythmic content. Observe the four following examples which illustrate types of rhythm: (a) active rhythm; (b) varied phrase pattern; (c) groups with similar rhythm; and (d) groups with dissimilar rhythm.

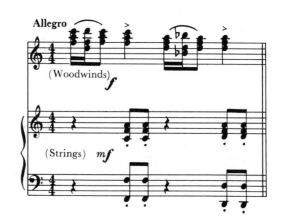

Any number of groups may be added together if each has its own harmonic completeness and if together they have an effective rhythmic co-ordination. Because of their somewhat limited ranges, trumpets and horns will often be in close harmony, depending upon the expressive intensity needed.

As long as the very strongly unifying force of the chordal texture is in action almost any spacing or pitch emphasis will have some special flavor or interest. Spacing, choice of register, and the amount of doubling of the third are almost entirely matters of personal preference, but a certain consistency of voice leading is nearly always desirable. In this next example, the third has been included in each choir. Since each choir is harmonically consistent and complete, the sound is effective.

Observe the following points in Schumann's organization or harmony:

Close harmony in the brasses is balanced by open harmony in the strings.

The groups are each harmonically complete within themselves.

A certain light and shade is achieved by differing design within each choir.

In the main, the differing instruments utilize their natural registers.

133

from SCHUMANN: *Symphony No. 1 in B-flat Major,* "Spring"

Sibelius features low string harmony in order to let the woodwinds through. Brahms often seems to prefer a certain close harmonic concentration in the mellow middle register (bassoons, clarinets, violas), with the upper and lower parts of the texture open. Berlioz seems fond of a concentrated high-sounding harmony, with the middle registers rather open. Beethoven likes his woodwinds harmonically rich, but keeps the strings and brass more open in sound. What type of spacing do *you* prefer?

Project 3

Write a number of brief examples illustrating chordal texture. Begin with the natural spacing of any trio or quartet
combination and continue the spacing consistently through a
short chorale-like phrase; for example,

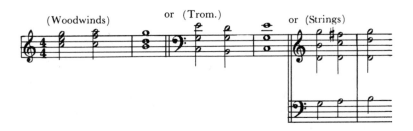

Following this, experiment with the combination of two or
three groups at once or write a short freely experimental composition in chordal texture for any available performing group.
Whenever possible, divide the instruments into choirs of similar
timbre, but if only a few mixed instruments are available, divide
them into any groupings for which one of the commonly used
spacings is practicable.

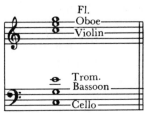

Beginners in composition should keep the rhythms hymn-
like and uniform in the two groups. Those with more experience
in composition technique may attempt some of the rhythmic
variety and motor interest suggested in the general discussion on
chordal texture.

Almost any standard masterwork will have some manifestation of chordal texture. Find several instances of chordal texture and analyze the harmonic spacings used.

Polyphonic Texture

To aid theoretical understanding it is important to point out, again, that the organizing power of the several textures comes from their ability to create types of unity. The primitively simple line unity of the monophonic texture and the concentrated vertical simultaneity of the chordal texture are easy to observe and acknowledge as sources of unity. The source of unity of the polyphonic texture is perhaps less immediately apparent.

Polyphonic means "many-voiced" when it is literally translated, but in musical terminology it has come to imply a similarity of pace and motion in the "many voices." The unity of the polyphonic texture could be compared to that of dramatic action upon a stage onto which twins, brothers, or other recognizably similar characters enter at different times and by different doors.

In polyphonic texture, the unity results from the several lines which are nearly similar but which enter and leave the musical fabric constantly, to create an overlapping action of several simultaneously continuing voices. The clarity results from the fusion of the several voices into a single impression. There is a dominating similarity of design presented by the overlapping action, which draws attention to motival or linear characteristics shared by all voices as they enter anew.

from BRAHMS: *Piano Concerto No. 2 in B-flat Major* (Baron)

PLATE II. CHORDAL TEXTURE

Nothing sounds more warmly sonorous and firmly clear than good polyphony. However, before examples are written for performance, the essential values of polyphonic texture must be clearly understood. Three or four strongly melodic lines sounding simultaneously are not necessarily polyphonic. Unless there is enough open space (sculptured silence) in each of the parts, unless the voices enter and leave the musical fabric by turn, and unless beats other than the first beat of the measure are highlighted as points of entry, the effect will be only partially successful as polyphony.

Every outstanding composer, from Bach to Webern, has used the polyphonic texture in orchestration. It is timeless and absolutely basic. It can contain any reasonable number of authentic voices, but the composer will learn early that a structure made up of only two or three strong lines can have amazing interest and clarity when projected by orchestral sound.

Polyphonic lines may be in unison or octaves, and choice will be determined by the amount of power desired. For variety, some lines may be in unison while others are doubled in octaves. Choice of timbre is an entirely personal matter, but variety is of great importance. Too continuous use of timbre of any one kind may result in monotony. On the other hand, a too frequent change of timbre may result in a rather "scrappy" sound.

Sometimes a too prolonged use of pure polyphony can become tiring because of lack of harmonic effect. To counter this, composers sometimes supplement the sound with a small amount of supporting harmony, motivally insignificant and usually limited to two or three voices.

Study the three examples on the next pages.

The amount of harmonic support given will depend upon personal taste and the dramatic or climactic need of the music. Although harmonic support adds warmth and substance, it also endangers the effectiveness of the polyphonic texture, the main glory of which is clean, clear, linear design.

(a) unison lines:

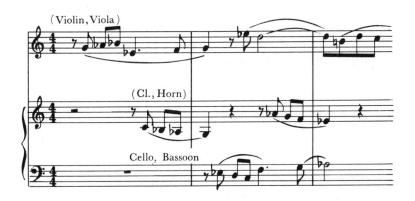

(b) lines in octaves:

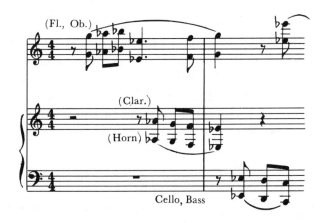

(c) mixed octave and unison lines with thin supporting harmony:

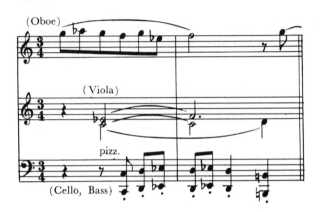

Project 4

Orchestrate any short phrase which employs the polyphonic texture. Use reduced scoring as in the three examples above, and try to achieve variety, melodic interest and growth. Apply varied timbre and sufficient octave doubling to contrast with unison line. Use sufficient register variegation. Study polyphonic sections in the works of various masters of orchestration (see the charts on pages 301–303). Examine the scoring methods used by Stokowski, Schönberg, Respighi, Webern and others in transcribing the music of Bach for orchestra.

Homophonic Texture

In each of the textures previously explained (monophonic, chordal and polyphonic), the unity of action resulted from *similarities* of line, rhythm and motion.

140

from KODÁLY: *Concerto for Orchestra* (Copyright 1942, Revised Edition 1958—reprinted by permission of Boosey & Hawkes, Inc.)

PLATE III. POLYPHONIC TEXTURE

The clarity of the homophonic texture results from *differentiation* of the instrumental action into three functional elements: (a) melody, (b) accompanimental rhythmic design, and (c) sustaining chord. The more positively these elements are differentiated, the clearer the resulting orchestration will be.

It is this combination of differing action in the homophonic texture that dominates page after page of the orchestration of Rimsky-Korsakov and also the many illustrative examples in his treatise on orchestration. Observe the contrast of roles in this example, from his *Scheherazade*:

Although this balance of roles has been associated with much commonplace Romantic Period music, it is misleading to suppose that all homophonic music is necessarily dull. The homophonic texture represents, in fact, the most complete and subtle of all orchestral balances, and it has been constantly used with marvelous elaboration and ramification in the orchestration of imaginative composers such as Debussy, Ravel, Prokofiev and others.

It has been a fundamental resource through all style periods

and, in various manifestations, has been used more than any
other orchestral texture.

If balanced by significant melody and adequate harmony,
the rhythmic accompanimental material is free to expand into
expression and design of great interest. This potentiality for
freshness and inventiveness in the accompanimental material is
a constant challenge to ingenuity and motor sensibility.

The homophonic texture is not really as old-fashioned as is
sometimes implied by those who reject it in favor of more "contemporary" types. Since the homophonic clarity results from a
more developed and subtle perception (an understanding of the
value of contrast), it represents a mental advance toward structural awareness. Homophonic texture will therefore remain as
a major factor in music.

To maintain a balance of textures, a composer might well
alternate homophonic texture with the other more primitively
simple (monophonic, chordal and polyphonic) types.

In writing for performance, a few variants in the application of the homophonic texture should be kept in mind.

For example, an accompanimental pattern sometimes combines both the motion and sustaining factors into one compound
design.

Sometimes the melody may be expanded into a harmonized line. Such reinforced melody is still a sufficient line in terms of the definition of homophonic texture (contrast of line, sustaining material, and accompanimental pattern). Study the three versions of a line given in this example:

or

or

The more harmonic the line becomes, the less harmonic the accompanimental pattern will need to be.

Sometimes a homophonic texture will include what is commonly called a *counter-melody*. As it relates to the main melody, it is roughly contrapuntal and by itself is melodically incomplete. It must merge into the melodic action without drawing too much attention to itself.

Project 5

Write examples to illustrate homophonic texture. Take special care to assure that your design plan positively differentiates the three "roles" (melodic line, rhythmic accompanimental design, and chordal sustaining material). In the sustaining choir, chords do not always need to be full; sometimes a single sustained tone will suffice. Use percussion freely, as it is very

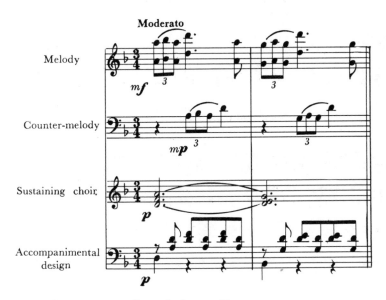

from SCHUBERT: *Serenade* (arranged)

effective as part of the accompanimental pattern and can even simulate sustaining effect by continuing the sounds of timpani and certain gongs and cymbals with a "roll" (by using soft sticks).

For concentrated practice use four staves, as in the above example. This will keep the contrasted action of the basic elements clearly before you as scoring proceeds.

Polythematic Texture

The unity of the polythematic texture also results from a vivid and intentional *differentiation,* but this differentiation is derived from a contrast of motival opposites, simultaneously interacting. This requires a positive contrast of architectural characteristics in two or more lines of motival action which will

145

from BARTÓK: *Piano Concerto No.* 3 (Copyright 1947 by Boosey & Hawkes Ltd.—reprinted by permission of Boosey & Hawkes, Inc.)

PLATE IV. HOMOPHONIC TEXTURE

pit curve against angle, leaping energy against steadiness, agitation and rapidity against calm, *staccato* against *legato*, or fullness against thinness, etc.

Since it offers such an opportunity for live and interesting use of the various motor characteristics of the instruments, the polythematic texture is being used more and more in modern orchestration.

In the nineteenth and twentieth centuries the mechanisms of the brasses, woodwinds and percussion were greatly improved, and the playing ability of the average orchestra player increased markedly. It is natural, therefore, that modern composers should be keenly interested in new potentialities for technical manipulation. This interest in instrumental motion for its own sake has led to an emphasis on polythematic texture.

There should be no "dead" parts in polythematism, for to be successfully characteristic this texture requires strong and vivid motival design at all times. For this reason it can be especially meaningful to the players.

Observe this moment of polythematic texture (motival contrast) from the *Symphony No. 6* by Beethoven:

In this example both motives are written for sections of string tone. It is more usual, however, for the polythematic contrast to occur between contrasting timbres—as in this quote from the *Concerto for Violin and Orchestra* by Tchaikovsky:

147

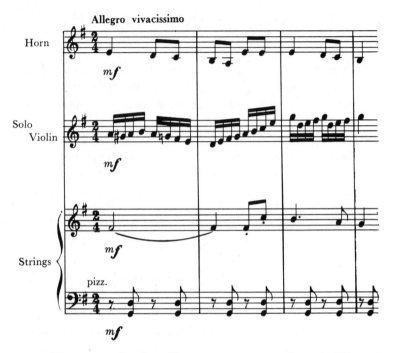

This example also illustrates contrasts of pace. The solo violin is active and fast moving, the horn is more moderate in its tempo, *tutti* violins are more leisurely and *legato*, and the *pizzicato* accompaniment is neutral.

Usually two such live motives on a given page are quite enough for the average listener. If a third motive is brought into the texture, it must necessarily be rather inconspicuous and be inclined toward the non-motival character of accompanimental material. In the example on p. 149, which of the three motives is the most definite? Which is the least definite or most like accompanimental material?

Project 6

In preparing for experimentation with polythematic texture it is helpful to practice invention of motival ideas for each of the

separate instruments of the orchestra. Each instrument has potentialities for characteristic motion that are individual to it alone, and which can be produced only by its particular playing techniques. The scores of Stravinsky, Debussy, Rimsky-Korsakov and Berlioz are outstanding for their exemplification of the musical interest that can naturally result when the instruments are set into motion by designs that make the most of idiomatic potentialities. The scores of Stravinsky are particularly inventive in this direction and should be studied for the stimulating examples they afford.

After preliminary exercise in the invention of idiomatic motives and designs for each instrument, try combining some of them into polythematic textures. Or, after you have become interested in some particular motival effect, search mentally for another that will add contrast and supplementary strength to it.

Keep in mind that both motival tangibility and motival contrast are essential to the polythematic textural values. Paradoxically, successful unity and variety both result from such definiteness within contrast. For architectural contrast, pit *stac-*

149

from RUBBRA: *Symphony No. 5* (Lengnick)

PLATE V. POLYTHEMATIC TEXTURE

cato against *legato*, angle against curve, smooth motion against angular or disjointed motion, etc. Usually a contrast of basic pace between the opposing motives is desirable. A rapid and agitated motion should ordinarily be contrasted by one that is more moderate and slow.

In the Tchaikovsky example on page 148, a slight amount of accompanimental material was also added. If such accompanimental or sustaining material is included it must be kept particularly slight in motival content, lest it spoil the impact of the polythematism, which ordinarily has the most strength and clarity when limited to two strong motival elements.

Polyrhythmic Texture

The characteristic unity of the polyrhythmic texture results from a dominating rhythmic "drive," or unified kinesthetic impact, which enables the listener to merge differing threads of instrumental motion into a single impression.

There can be quite a number of simultaneous but differentiated threads in this composite, but the action of each of these threads of motion must be non-motival, so that no one motion factor will predominate. Within an excitingly primitive rhythmic emphasis, an overriding similarity of "beat" will absorb and unify an idiomatic and rhythmic diversity.

The polyrhythmic texture, with its interplay of variety and unity and its almost hypnotic rhythmic excitement, originates from a time as far back as it is possible to trace African drums and other orgiastic percussions.

Although common to ancient and primitive music, polyrhythm became almost extinct in the music of the Classic and Romantic Periods. It has had a revival in the music of twentieth-century composers such as Stravinsky and Debussy. It also has had an influence on jazz music. The modern use of polyrhythmic texture grew partially from a widening of musical expression to include a certain primitive energy drawn from attractively naïve folk cultures.

Analyze the opening pages of Stravinsky's *Petrouchka*—with its exciting "hurly-burly" of instrumental action. Also study the opening pages of *Ibéria* by Debussy and certain passages in his *La Mer* that tend toward the polyrhythmic. The example below exemplifies the characteristics of the polyrhythmic texture.

Project 7

Write a page of polyrhythmic score. Start by inventing a particularly active rhythmic pattern, for any instrument or for any thinly harmonized unit of similar timbre. Combine this with other thinly harmonized or single-line rhythmic patterns which will contribute variety and interest but which will merge naturally into the rhythmic unity of the basic "beat."

The concentrated rhythmic focus of the polyrhythmic texture can cause it to become monotonous after a short time, unless there is some element of variety. There may have to be some vestige of melody, thematic interest or phrase continuity, but these should be kept at a minimum, so that the over-all impression of exciting motor action will dominate the musical effect.

Heterophonic Texture

The word "heterophonic" when literally translated means "with differentiated voices." When applied to orchestration, it implies a principal melodic line sounding with other concurrent lines which are recognizably similar yet different enough to create internal surprise and variety. The heterophonic texture could be said to be "a melody with simultaneous variations."

One or more such simultaneous variations may be added, depending upon the degree of complexity desired. In the following two examples, the variations are more complex than the melody to which they are added.

This and the next example from BEETHOVEN: *Violin Concerto in D Major*

The variation added is often more simple than the melody, rather than more complex. If more than one variation is added, a certain balance between simplicity and complexity is desirable. If it has sufficient unity and enough surprise and variety of motion, the resulting heterophonic effect will be both clear and interesting.

Primitive peoples made much use of heterophonic techniques. These techniques are naturally effective in any essentially monodic music, and still furnish great vitality and excitement when applied to the modern orchestra.

from MALIPIERO: *Impressioni dal Vero* (By permission of the copyright owners, J. & W. Chester, Ltd., London)

PLATE VI. POLYRHYTHMIC TEXTURE

155

The heterophonic texture is mainly a melodic phenomenon. Therefore, if harmony is added it should be kept quite thin. Accompanimental material will ordinarily not be needed, since the varied action of the other voices supplies enough complexity of motion.

However, when elaborating the accompaniment in homophonic design there is a special heterophonic technique which can be applied. The example on page 154 shows an accompanimental unit which has been heterophonically enriched by differing versions of an essentially arpeggiated motion.

Analyze the relationship of the voices in the next example. Which variant of the melody is more complex? Which is more simple? Would you add harmony or further accompanimental design?

The type of heterophonic texture thus far illustrated and explained can be designated as *horizontal heterophony*.

There is another type of simultaneous heterphonic texture which can be designated as *vertical heterophony*. In this textural manifestation two more or less familiar and self-sufficient tunes are played at the same time (vertically juxtaposed), e.g., *Swanee River* by Foster and *Humoresque* by Dvořák. The impression of unity results from the natural clarity of meaning of the readily recognized tunes. The polyphony will be rough, harsh, and perhaps incorrect, but the resulting variety will have an attractively vigorous and rough-hewn quality of unique interest.

The tunes are heterophonically related because they are positively "differing voices."

A well-known example of this *vertical* application of heterophony occurs in Wagner's *Die Meistersinger* Overture, at the point where the composer finally brings together three main motives which have previously been heard separately—shown in the reproduction below. Each of these is memorably tuneful. They are rather similar in motion, but different enough to make sufficient variety in combination.

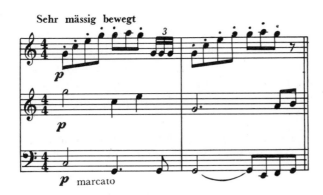

Still another illustration is this moment in the Shostakovitch *Symphony No. 1.* Here the first and second themes have been brought together. Each is authentically tuneful in its own right. Note the rough-hewn vigor of the design and the independence of the harmony (see example on page 158).

Project 8

Write some pages of reduced scoring to illustrate the two types of heterophonic texture (horizontal and vertical). In the

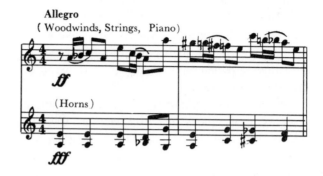

horizontal type, try for intensity of motor interest. In the vertical type, the page will probably be limited to the lines of the independent tunes. Because the differing lines will have already put such a strain on the attention, other demands can hardly be added without endangering clarity. Study scores and search out as many examples as you can of heterophonic texture types. Observe the necessarily stark and linear character of the design, also the relative sparseness of sustaining and accompanimental material.

Good heterophonic examples may be found in the *Lieutenant Kijé* Suite by Prokofiev and in "Farandole" from the *L'Arlésienne* Suite by Bizet.

Onomatopoeic Texture

The word *onomatopoeic* implies "imitation of natural sounds." If the composer brings in an actual cuckoo call, as Beethoven did in the "Pastoral" Symphony, or as Delius did in *On Hearing the First Cuckoo in Spring*, the effect may be said to be "onomatopoeic."

When orchestration employs such literal portrayal or is strongly programmatic, the resulting unity creates an "onomatopoeic" texture.

158

from PROKOFIEV: *Lieutenant Kijé* Suite (Copyright by Edition A. Gutheil, copyright assigned 1947 to Boosey & Hawkes, Inc.—reprinted by permission)

PLATE VII. HETEROPHONIC TEXTURE (differing versions of the same musical idea sounding simultaneously)

159

from PROKOFIEV: *Lieutenant Kijé* Suite (Copyright by Edition A. Gutheil, copyright assigned 1947 to Boosey & Hawkes, Inc.—reprinted by permission)

PLATE VIII. HETEROPHONIC TEXTURE (independent tunes sounding simultaneously)

When Respighi causes a "fountain of sound" to rise and fall in the score of *The Fountains of Rome*, or when, by use of a phonograph, he brings the actual song of the nightingale into the score of *The Pines of Rome*, or when he has the trombones imitating the roar of the lions in *Roman Festivals*, the music has a texture that may be said to be "onomatopoeic."

Such a texture is not easily definable in terms of architecture, except to say that the resulting shapes and patterns reflect the contours and motions of nature.

It is the dramatic verity of these contours and motions that convinces the listener and gives meaning to what might otherwise be a chaotic, monotonous or random musical experience.

A composer might write a piece called "Chaos No. 1," or "Turbulence No. 2," or a single smashing sound to be entitled "A Punch in the Nose"; if the audience were dramatically convinced, mere chaotic motion, random turbulent action, or sudden savage impact would be seemingly clear and meaningful.

Sometimes a score will combine onomatopoeic patterns with more structurally clear textural prototype, as in *The Ride of the Valkyries* by Wagner (essentially homophonic).

Project 9

Attempt a page of story-telling orchestration. In addition to the Respighi scores already mentioned, analyze others such as *Impressioni dal Vero* by Malipiero (the owl, the woodpecker, cypresses, etc.), *Peter and the Wolf* by Prokofiev, certain sections of *Pictures at an Exhibition* by Moussorgsky (orchestrated by Ravel), and *Pacfic 231* by Honegger. Attempt to imitate sounds and actions from everyday life: children at play, machines at work, church bells ringing, waterfront sounds, and so on. It is said that Leoš Janáček frequented the market place to write down actual speech sounds to be used in his music. The relation of Sibelius' *Tapiola* to the arctic winds and forests is movingly clear.

from RESPIGHI: *The Fountains of Rome* (By permission of G. Ricordi & Co., copyright owner)

PLATE IX. ONOMATOPOEIC TEXTURE

Textural Combination

Control over group organization and the ability to invent clear and positive texture types are basic to any soundly developed orchestration technique. Other principles of clarity will be studied subsequently, but the techniques of unit consistency and texture formation should be thoroughly understood and practiced before going on.

Throughout all future stages of orchestration study, it will be important to analyze scores constantly to observe the formative power of the textural prototypes. Such analysis will keep alive an understanding of the creative force and organizing power of these elemental unities. They must be understood as protean sources, structurally necessary to any textural manifestation.

All discussions thus far have presented textures in their most elemental forms, but as scores are analyzed it will be discovered that there are many variants of these fundamental types. Through compounding and hybridization, many transformations of the basic unities are possible.

A *compound* texture is a texture with two or more choirs, each of which is organized according to a different principle of unity. In the example opposite from (Franck's *Symphony in D Minor*), the composer has organized the horns as a chordal texture. At the same time the trumpets and trombones together make a polyphonic texture.

A *hybrid* texture is a texture that blends the characteristics of two different unities. For instance, there might be two essentially chordal textures, one in woodwind and one in brass, overlapping in a polyphonic way:

Why is this chordal? Why is it polyphonic? Why is it not a compound texture?

These possibilities of compounding and hybridization are endless, and further study in orchestration could well include experiments with these complex types. Keep in mind, however, that the closer texture comes to the pure prototype, the stronger its impact will be and the more immediately intelligible it will be to the audience. Before attempting complex textures, succeed first with the simple ones.

At this point in the development of technical understanding it is pertinent to re-emphasize that the choice of timbre or "tone color" is very much a matter of personal preference. There is no need to be overly concerned yet about choice of timbre; clarity of structure comes first. If the groups are consistent and the textures positive, almost any timbre takes on a fascinatingly mysterious quality.

Certainly, choice of tone color makes a real difference and is, in a way, the very heart of orchestration; but achievement of clarity should come first in the earlier stages of study.

PITCH DISTRIBUTION

The placement of tones into effective pitch locales has much to do with clarity. Melodies, accompaniments and harmonies must be placed in the registers in which they can be most clearly heard in relation to one another. Extremely high pitches tend to obscure lower tones. Extremely low tones are difficult to hear clearly and produce a blurred effect when used harmonically. Middle register tones are weak and easily obscured.

On the staff there is a central area located among the tones closest to middle C—see the example below. This is the tonal area that is most inconspicuous and the most naturally suited to accompanimental design and harmonic background. It is in this register that the horns, violas, clarinets and second violins seem to be comfortably non-stringent, normally relaxed and fluent. When written higher, accompanimental material takes on brightness and shrillness; and when written lower, harmonies become progressively blurred and vague as the lowest tones are approached.

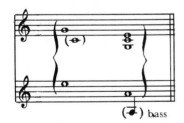

Normal accompanimental distribution

Competing factors in similar pitch locale have a tendency to neutralize one another and to obliterate design. When melody,

165

accompaniment and harmony, or competing motives and lines are located in different non-competing pitch locales, the result is crystal-clear and vivid.

To illustrate the negative action of two motives competing in the same register, let us suppose that there are two motival designs in two different tone colors sounding together as follows:

Because they are in the same register, neither motive can be heard clearly, since the two tend to "eat each other up." At one time or another, every novice composer will have suffered from this ineffective sort of distribution of registers. One way to improve the result would be to move the violins up an octave, so that the trumpets can have the middle register to themselves. Or, if the trumpet design were played by flutes, an octave higher, the violins could continue in middle register with typical D-string vigor. In either case, the design could come forth clearly. Because of this attention to the pitch locale, the two opposing designs would no longer interfere with one another.

The shrill intensity of extreme high pitch or the gruff "fogginess" of extreme low pitch becomes tiring if allowed to continue for too long. If both high and low pitches sound together for any length of time, the danger to clarity is further increased.

The foregoing analyses lead to the following general recommendations for the restriction and control of pitch distribution:

(a) Use the natural and moderate middle register much of the time, alone or in combination with either high or low pitch.

(b) Use high and low pitch together (without middle register) only for special effect.

(c) Use the high, middle and low pitches, sounding together, only for maximum intensity and only for brief periods of time.

(d) High pitch alone or low pitch alone is very expressive but incomplete and tiring.

(e) Competing motival ideas should be in different registers.

(f) There should be sufficient variegation of pitch locale to ensure growth, variety and interest.

When a certain composer said "All symphony orchestras scream," he was, no doubt, thinking of the tendency of composers of the Romantic Period to overuse the high brilliant sounds for dramatic excitement.

There is an acoustical fact back of this observation. High frequencies tend to absorb and obscure low frequencies when they are sounded together. This means that the addition of low sounds to high will enrich the high sounds, but the addition of too many high sounds to low will tend to block out the low sounds. If low sounds are to be featured they should be heard in a rather isolated structure. What registers would you choose for the accompaniment in a concerto for double bass?

Project 10

Write a page of score which will demonstrate effective use of pitch distribution. Illustrate: (a) sufficient use of middle register; (b) clarity of motival content through pitch differentiation of competing motives; (c) surprise, change and climax through alternation of high, low and middle register; and (d) limited use of extremes of high and low pitch.

CREATIVE ORCHESTRATION

from DEBUSSY: *Ibéria* (Permission for reprint granted by Durand et Cie, Paris, France, copyright owners; Elkan-Vogel Co., Inc., Philadelphia, Pa., agents)

PLATE X. PITCH DISTRIBUTION

168

The music of Debussy, Mozart, Mendelssohn and Tchai-kovsky shows evidence of conscious control of pitch distribution for clarity. Study the works of these masters for analysis of the relation of pitch locale to clarity (see the charts on pp. 301–303).

LIMITATION OF HARMONY

Orchestral instruments are so naturally rich in overtones that when they are sounded together harmonic effects are in-tensified. Even when played in unison there is an illusion of harmony. The harmonies in the score will seem magnified in performance, so that harmonization which is too full will en-danger structural clarity.

Study of scores will lead to the conclusion that master com-posers often restrict the harmony in order to allow essential design to come through clearly.

The music of Beethoven is typical of this kind of restriction. It serves especially well as a general illustration of the effective limitation of harmony, and it shows the importance of such limi-tation to the achievement of the clearest possible result.

The outstanding clarity of the music of Beethoven seems to imply a formula for harmonic limitation which may be stated as follows: (a) in the string section use strong, clear, linear design with a very small amount of harmony in the middle regis-ter; (b) restrict the brass to strong, open, foundational intervals; (c) concentrate the harmonic emphasis in the woodwinds, where it will be most softened and inconspicuous.

Observe the application of this formula in this excerpt from the *Symphony No. 6* of Beethoven (p. 170).

It is when played by the brass choir that harmony has the most naturally intense harmonic impact. If the harmonization is located there, hardly more will be needed, especially since additional harmony in the woodwinds and strings can be heard

only with difficulty. If all three choirs are harmonic at the same time, the effect will be too full, too cloying and too undifferentiated.

Even when the harmony is limited to the brass, care must be taken not to fill up too wide a total range with brass timbre, as this will tend to obstruct the possibility for other timbres to be clearly heard.

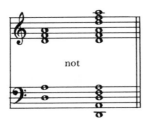

not

Most other composers do not concentrate the harmony in the woodwind section as Beethoven did. More often, they alternate the harmonic role among the several choirs (even percussion can simulate harmony with bell sounds). Beethoven's treatment of harmony was an outcome of his personal predilection, and it should not be imitated too exactly; but it does prove, through the outstanding clarity of his music, the general value of limitation of harmony.

If three degrees of harmonic intensity are categorized into: (1) close harmony (strongly harmonic), (2) foundational open harmony (moderately harmonic), and (3) linear design (nonharmonic), a general law may be stated as follows:

The most normal balance in the use of harmony will result from a combination of three different degrees of harmonic intensity.

The three different degrees (strong, moderate and nonharmonic) should be distributed among differing families of sound.

Six optional distributions are possible, since these three degrees of intensity can be combined in six different ways.

TABLE I

1. Woodwind (close)	Brass (open)	Strings (linear)
2. Woodwind (close)	Brass (linear)	Strings (open)
3. Woodwind (open)	Brass (linear)	Strings (close)
4. Woodwind (open)	Brass (close)	Strings (linear)
5. Woodwind (linear)	Brass (close)	Strings (open)
6. Woodwind (linear)	Brass (open)	Strings (close)

Any one of these distributions of the harmonic emphasis would produce an effective balance of harmonic intensity or, in other words, a *normal harmonic limitation*.

Project 11

Write some pages of reduced scoring in which experiments are directed toward trying out various dispositions of the harmonic factor. Balance the differing degrees of intensity as suggested by the previous discussion and table of balances.

For the best harmonic result certain other points about harmony should be kept in mind:

(a) When played on a piano, quick changes of complex harmony are easily and clearly heard, but if harmonies change rapidly in orchestral music they are more difficult to follow. Orchestra harmony, therefore, needs to be based upon a slower harmonic rhythm than does harmony for other media.

(b) Orchestral harmony normally maintains a consistency of choir action (number of voices and type of spacing), but the number of voices and type of spacing may be varied if varied within a design which is sufficiently clear and purposeful.

(c) The relation of parallel, oblique and contrary motion should be balanced. At any point in harmonic progression where there are two or more choirs there will be a need for supplementary difference. If all choirs move upward or downward at the same time there will be an imbalance which, if continued over a long period, could make both players and audience "seasick" with parallel motion.

Since the orchestra is such a massive entity, orchestral music needs some kind of "keel" action at the center of things, so that parallel and contrary motion in other groups can be steadied or stabilized by their relation to it.

Play the following parallel structure:

Play it again, this time with a stabilizing or "keel" action added by the horns. Note the increased strength and interest in the effect.

In further scoring, a unit of contrary motion might be added. This would give still more stability and balance.

Since the very essence of value in orchestration is design and movement, harmony is perhaps only a lesser or minor element, which often becomes stronger in effect than was intended. Young composers sometimes dote upon the harmony which they conjure up from the piano and use improvisation as a resource from which to evoke intensity of feeling. In writing for orchestra this tendency must be somewhat guarded against for the sake of strong design. Harmony can be magnificently poignant and expressive, as Delius, Wagner and Franck prove by their music. Nevertheless, it is suggested that for healthy growth in the study of orchestration the highest aim should be flourishing design in combination with somewhat meager harmony—not the opposite (flourishing harmony with meager design) which is often the "easiest way."

One of the great surprises to the orchestrator when he first hears one of his scores played in actuality will be how much less vivid his choice harmonies and dissonances will be than he expected if he writes in an exaggeratedly harmonic manner. The sound of the orchestra tends to flatten out or absorb harmonies and to jumble them if there is a too rapid harmonic rhythm. On the other hand exciting motion and clear design are more nearly magnified and there are even illusions of harmonic richness that can come from the overtones suggested by simple lines and the sensuous response aroused by timbre in vivid motion.

As you gain experience in scoring you will more and more come to understand that creativity in orchestration is more essentially the invention of motion and design and it would be good experience to invent purely abstract charts of sounds in motion and then transfer these patterns to actual sound without much reference to conventional harmony. When there are instruments present in the laboratory situation, students should improvise freely together with random harmony but vivid motion and design. It often will result in astounding colorfulness and design interest.

from COPLAND: *Appalachian Spring* (Copyright 1945 by Hawkes & Son [London] Ltd.—reprinted by permission)

PLATE XI. LIMITATION OF HARMONY

VIVIDNESS OF TIMBRE

A melody or pattern is strengthened and made clearer when it is presented to the ear by means of a vivid timbre. When timbre is non-vivid, structural elements have a tendency to be absorbed into the general background.

Vividness can be partially achieved by loudness or softness, but the most intense vividness results only from distinctive tonal character. Unusual timbre is sometimes inherent, as in the case of the English horn, which always makes a striking effect with its dark, brooding tone. However, unusual timbre is most often obtained by the use of extreme registers (high or low).

Nearly every instrument is rather mild and neutral in its middle register. The clarinet is a typical example of this, in its middle register it is easily obscured and relatively simple in sound, but in its upper register it takes on a brightness and positiveness of character which is shrilly and sweetly intense. The low or *chalumeau* register is rich, warm and dramatic, and it has a distinctive character that cannot be duplicated by any other instrument or register. The viola and cello also become characteristically vivid in high or low register, while becoming more neutral in the middle register.

These differences naturally suggest the use of middle register for background material when the aim is to effect a sort of quiet obscurity. If the aim is to vivify soloistic or motival material, high or low registers should be used.

In performing groups in which all voices have relatively similar timbre (e.g., the male chorus and the string orchestra), it is difficult to clarify design by means of vividness of timbre. This means that in these media special attention should be given to structural methods of ensuring clarity. The symphonic band, the mixed-voice choral groups and the pipe organ have a less oppressive similarity of timbre than the male chorus and string orchestra, but they, too, must depend principally upon structural means for clarity or upon conscious use of strikingly opposed registers. In the band, the sound is too often neutrally bland because of the constant sounding together of brass and woodwind. When the brass and woodwind are antiphonally separated, the sound immediately becomes more vivid and therefore clearer.

Opportunities for clarification through the use of vivid timbres are naturally offered by the orchestra because of its variety of tone color resources unequalled by any other medium. This vast palette of tone is a natural challenge to experimentation.

Timbre becomes more vivid when highlighted by essential contrast. In Table II, a few types of tone quality are listed in contrasting pairs.

TABLE II

Dry	(snare drum, *pizzicato* strings)
Liquid	(glockenspiel, flute, clarinet)
Sibilant	(rattle, flute fluttertongue)
Solid	(wood-block, xylophone, trumpet)
Mellow	(viola, low clarinet)
Harsh	(trombone fluttertongue, cymbal crash)

Other contrasts which might be categorized for possible use are smooth–sharp, brittle–plastic, ethereal–vulgar, shrill–mellow, etc.

177

Categorization of tonal contrast is technically difficult and is a relatively unexplored psychological realm, as is evidenced by the groping terminology that must be used to describe tone qualities. Surprisingly little is said about timbre contrast in the literature of musical analysis. The unexplored world of percussion timbre has been especially neglected. There has not been a positive enough attempt to classify timbre according to the "attributes of tone" (the scientific term used by psychologists). Since timbre contrast is of such importance to the art of orchestration, perhaps the future will bring psychological clarification and a more positive terminology.

Although this categorization is a psychologist's scientific problem, it is nevertheless a musical artist's practical problem which must be met, in spite of the present lack of scientifically established terminology. Practical experiments with timbre contrast will lead to the following general principle:

> *Opposing timbres in differing design tend to become particularly clear.*

For example, a trumpet or xylophone sounding against a background of middle-range strings would effect a contrast of strident against subdued tone. Or, a *pizzicato* line in the strings against a choir of flute sound would effect a contrast of dryness against liquidity.

Project 12

Write examples in reduced scoring which illustrate the clarifying effect of vividness of timbre. Speculate into the nature of the "attributes of tone" and try out some contrasts that come to mind. Contrast of any kind will be increasingly recognized as a central orchestral resource almost as fruitful as orderly design in ensuring clarity.

The world of percussion sound, in particular, has a wealth of fascinating timbres that invite exploration. After hearing some percussion works of composers such as Chávez and Varèse, make experiments of your own in the use of percussion timbre. Increase your knowledge about the percussive "attributes of tone" by trying out various opposites. Use duo combinations of pure percussion, or duo combinations which combine percussive and sustained timbres.

LIMITATION OF MELODIC COMPONENTS

In music, some elements of design require very little attention for comprehension. Because they are simple in structure, briefly stated and repeated, they are intelligible almost immediately. Other elements of design are more lengthy and without repetition. They acquire their meanings from a set of consecutive relationships which may be compared to those of syntax in a sentence.

It is this relation of words or musical symbols that demands attention and mental effort. In language, this consecutive meaning results in the sentence. In music it becomes the melodic line, theme, motive or phrase.

If a succession of words without syntax is presented to the attention, as in the statement "rain, rain, rain," little effort is needed for comprehension and the mind can pass on to something else. However, if an elaborate syntax is presented, as in the statement "because of certain low pressure systems converging from the south, it will probably begin raining today at 2 P.M.; there will be some snow and hail, and you had better carry chains in the car," closer attention is required.

Music is similar to language since it demands varying degrees of concentration. Analyze the following rhythmic pattern. The musical meaning is easily comprehended because the statement of the design is contained in a single measure and from TCHAIKOVSKY: *Nutcracker Suite* (Kalmus)

PLATE XII. VIVIDNESS OF TIMBRE

this measure is repeated. It is intentionally relaxed and non-consecutive in its meaning.

If this same material is developed so that it takes on a set of consecutive relationships, it must be heard throughout its length because of an organic totality which requires concentrated attention. If it is to be comprehended, more mental effort must be expended.

In orchestration, those elements which contain this more demanding consecutive meaning can be spoken of as *melodic components*. To achieve clarity in orchestration, there must be limitation in the number of melodic components sounding at any one time.

The memory and the attention power of the average listener are limited. It seems that the average mind can follow only one train of thought thoroughly at a time. To illustrate this, a comparison can be made to an attention-distracting situation from real life. If a person is asked to give attention to several things at once (a telephone conversation which is in progress, a political speech blaring over the radio, a scolding landlady, the town crier passing by), he will either grasp only fragments of each or will have to block out the others and give attention to the one that he really wants to comprehend.

In music, the psychological facts are comparable to those just described. The average listener can follow only one line of consecutive musical thought (one melodic component) at a time. Psychological experiment leads to this conclusion.* The ability to grasp two (rarely three) melodic components sounding simultaneously can be developed only by those with intense musical training. Given a specific degree of natural or developed attention power, the progressive addition of simultaneously sounding melodic components rapidly increases the difficulty of comprehension to the point of impossibility.

Beethoven, with his gift for clarity, seems to apply this knowledge about the listener's powers. His orchestration shows an almost instinctive limitation of melodic components, and it rarely demands attention to more than one melodic component at any one time.

Study the scores of Beethoven to analyze this limitation of melodic demand. Choose any one of the Beethoven symphonies and go through the score, underlining melodic components at different points. This will supply a vivid visual exemplification of the principle of limitation of melodic components.

For maximum clarity an orchestral texture should contain only one melodic component. There can sometimes be two components, but the second should be less demanding in its consecutive content than the principal melodic component. If a third melodic component is added, it will necessarily be even more restricted to a minimal consecutive content.

The excerpt on p. 183, from the *Piano Concerto No. 2* by Brahms, will illustrate three levels of melodic definiteness and is an example of Brahms' limitation of melodic components.

After stating the foregoing formulation, questions will immediately arise. Polyphonic texture has three, four, five, or more

---

* Harrison E. McKay, "Multiple Tone-Pattern Discrimination" (Master's Thesis, Purdue University, 1958).

equally important voices—are these not melodic components? Polyrhythmic texture often has four, five or six threads of differentiated rhythmic action—are these not melodic components?

Let us answer these questions. In the polyrhythmic texture the purpose is a kind of "oneness" of over-all motion. The repetitive threads of design which merge into this "oneness" are not melodic components because they are intentionally non-consecutive and have the basic simplicity of accompanimental material. It seems that if the ear is not expected to hear any of the separate threads of musical action as consecutive thought, the whole composite of motion comes to the mind as one compound meaning. The result is a single merged impression.

The polyphonic texture usually has such similarity of motion in the voices that these also merge into a "oneness." A particularly characteristic quality of good polyphony is an "antiphonality" which permits the ear and attention to shift from one line to the other as principal motives come into the foreground, while lesser designs are comfortably absorbed into a generality of background motion. Any Bach fugue or invention will illustrate this alternating entrance of motive in polyphonic music, and will support the contention that a polyphonic texture is heard as one complex, developed, melodic component (a supreme example, of course, is his *Art of Fugue*).

The example on p. 185 is offered to illustrate the use of both polyphony and polyrhythm as components. The woodwinds are polyphonic (principal melodic component), the horns are polythematic (secondary melodic component), and the strings are polyrhythmic and non-melodic. There will still be an essential clarity when this compound texture is heard, because of the "oneness" of impression given by the unities of the polyphony and the polyrhythm.

As a final example to illustrate the need for limitation of melodic components, the illustration on p. 186 is offered from my own experience. In my *Evocation Symphony* (1951), there is a passage in the finale which was difficult to clarify in rehearsal.

Examination of the score will show that the rehearsal difficulty was caused by insufficient limitation of melodic components (even the tuba part has some small bit of consecutive meaning). The strings and horns are too similarly definite in melodic content, and the extremely active brass design also demands melodic attention. Since only *two* such attention-demanding elements can be successfully heard at one time, one of the three competing components will have to be modified. Either the brass has to be softened to *pianissimo*, so that it will become mere background, or the horn part has to be made less melodically definite, so that the listener can hear the string line and trumpet-trombone unit in combination as foreground.

Project 13

With the previous analyses in mind, plan some balances of melodic components which will fulfill the conditions necessary for clarity. On a page of reduced scoring, write first a principal

melodic component; then add a secondary component; finally, fill in a third musical element that makes only slight melodic demand (material that is sustaining or accompanimental in type).

This maintenance of balance of melodic components is a most important technique. If the study of orchestration had to be limited to only one guiding principle, limitation of melodic components might well be the best choice. Once the orchestrator has created the main melodic component and has added to it a secondary component, the essence of orchestration is in being. Further elaboration will usually be a mere filling in of decorative and supporting elements. Design of supporting elements and matters of pitch locale and tonal color are subject to freedom of choice and may be varied as personal preference indicates.

> But the need to achieve clarity through limitation of melodic components is fundamental to all orchestration.

Just as in life one cannot flout the laws of nature and physical health, so no real clarity is possible in orchestration without a reasonable limitation of the number of melodic components.

Study the works of some of the master composers (the three excerpts which follow are fine examples) and observe that, however complex the orchestral page may become, there will seldom be more than *two* melodic components used at any given time.

CONTROL OF DYNAMICS

Another important factor in the achievement of clarity is the calculation of dynamic balance. Even the clearest design can be destroyed and made incomprehensible if some instruments are playing too loudly. In orchestra performance, delicate sounds like the middle register of the clarinet, the muted trumpet or the sound of the harp, can be easily obliterated by other naturally

from BEETHOVEN: *Symphony No. 3 in E-flat Major, "Eroica"* (Kalmus)

PLATE XIII. LIMITATION OF MELODIC COMPONENTS

from BEETHOVEN: *Symphony No. 4 in B-flat Major* (Kalmus)

PLATE XIV. LIMITATION OF MELODIC COMPONENTS

from BEETHOVEN: *Symphony No. 5 in C minor* (Kalmus)

PLATE XV. LIMITATION OF MELODIC COMPONENTS

powerful timbres. A thundering timpani or drum roll can smother almost any other sound, and the *fortissimo* of the trumpets can wipe out all else like the "day of judgment." The woodwind section of the orchestra is particularly delicate when compared to the brass section, or when competing with a string group.

Conductors are constantly confronted with the need to achieve dynamic balance. There is an old story attributed to a Toscanini rehearsal. In going over a passage the conductor asked the bassoon player to play "more softly" and later, "still more softly." The bassoonist strove mightily but could not satisfy the conductor. Finally the player did not play at all and the conductor said, "Ah, just right!"

Control of dynamic factors requires a knowledge of the relative strength of tone of the various instruments. When the dynamic markings are precise, the impact of any design will be clarified. In a carefully marked score, timbres and groups will often be marked differently. Woodwinds may have to be marked *f* to balance brasses marked *p*. Similarly, it might be necessary to mark a clarinet in middle register *ff* to enable it to sound through (even when brasses are marked *p*).

There are certain balances that can be approximately calculated, such as the need for two French horns to balance the power of one trumpet or one trombone, but orchestral music varies so much in context and in use of registers that any "scientifically approximate" calculation of dynamics is not too trustworthy.

Experience will be the best teacher. As you hear your music performed (by any small laboratory group) you will encounter both surprise and disappointment. This will be the most effective kind of learning. Such experience in dynamic balancing should lead to more ability in controlling the dynamic factors with such markings as *forte, piano, sforzando, crescendo, diminuendo* and *marcato.*

The following general statements outline some of the more evident facts about dynamics:

(a) Trumpets and trombones are naturally powerful when open; when muted they are surprisingly weak.

(b) Woodwinds are easily overpowered by either the brasses or the full string group.

(c) Timpani and the military instruments (snare drum, bass drum and cymbal) are vigorously powerful and must be held in check.

(d) Middle-range clarinet is especially weak and can easily become obliterated.

(e) Harp, harpsichord and certain delicate percussions are weak and need to be brought forward.

(f) French horns are moderately strong and must sometimes be held in check.

(g) In full orchestra, strings playing *mf* may be considered the norm, or standard degree of dynamic intensity, against which the dynamics of other timbres must be balanced. Brasses and percussion are the strongest, while woodwinds are the weakest. In order to be heard in balance with strings marked *mf*, woodwinds should be marked *f*. In order to be heard in balance with the same strings, the brasses will ordinarily have to be marked *p*.

By the same token, if brasses are playing *mf*, strings will have to play *f* and woodwinds will have to play *ff*. Or, if woodwinds are playing *mf*, strings will have to play *p* to balance, while brasses must play *p* or *pp*.

Project 14

Experiment with control of dynamics by writing exercises especially planned to test the comparative power of the various instruments and the effect of dynamic marking on their balance. It is not necessary to write for the complete ensemble. A simple unison of two tones, an interval played by two instruments, or a chord played over and over with different indications, are perfectly suited to experiments in control of dynamics.

While attending orchestral concerts, pay particular attention to the sound of the orchestra in relation to the dynamics. If the conductor has balanced the dynamics in rehearsal, the music will be clear (provided it has been well written) and no design elements will be obscured. If, on the other hand, the design seems obscure and blurred, there has been either insufficient balancing of dynamics in rehearsal or lack of sufficient dynamic indications in the score.

Thus far in illustrating the principles of clarity, much potentially elaborate procedure has been expounded, but it must be emphasized that simplicity and directness are among the most desirable goals. It is particularly true of the large orchestra that a certain "epic" solidity and foundational resonance are necessary for good sound. This desirable strength and solidity can easily be lost when there is too much "fussiness" of design. In a long and elaborate composition the most wonderful moment may well be some particularly luminous sound or strong simple design. A page of score sounds twice as elaborate as it looks.

Experience will prove that there is a mysteriously creative effectiveness in inspired simple design—a kind of strength that no elaboration can equal. One of the surprises that should come early to the aspiring composer is the discovery that any characteristic instrumental timbre, if sounded in effective register and in clear design, will seem satisfying and mysteriously vital. There is a natural allurement conjured up by a skillfully produced tone. Nothing is more evocative, for example, than a simple oboe tone sustained in middle register. Add a touch of *pizzicato* and a natural attractiveness has been created!

from MAHLER: *Symphony No. 2 in C minor*, "Resurrection" (Kalmus)

PLATE XVI. CONTROL OF DYNAMICS

The survey of principles of clarity has now been completed. It is hoped that, as the result of exercises done thus far, clarity of design has become for you a natural and continuing outgrowth of your musical thought.

3

Principles of
Tonal Interest

WHAT MAKES FOR INTEREST OF TIMBRE HAS LONG BEEN somewhat of an unsolved mystery. Allurement and poetic poignance in sound have often been thought of as the inviolable province of the composer. In truth, the orchestration of a master such as Debussy does seem almost sublimely and frustratingly beyond the reach of rational explanation. Nevertheless, one of man's great achievements has been, and is, the gradual penetration into all mysteries by means of objective understanding; and the art of timbre, with its limitless iridescences, offers analytical challenges still to be met.

To explain completely the tonal poetry used by such geniuses of orchestration as Debussy or Stravinsky would be almost impossible, since it would require such a particularized and elaborate theory; but a beginning can be made by observing the action of certain fundamental processes and formulating them into practical principles.

Part of the "allure" of timbre comes from its association with types of motion and structure. Contrast also plays a very creative role in tone-mixing. Consciousness of register seems fundamental to choice of ingredients for tonal blend. When these three major sources (motion, contrast and register) are

197

studied as they combine into tonal phenomena, it will be noted that certain usages constantly recur. This frequent recurrence points to the existence of fundamental processes of creating timbre interest. These fundamental processes will now be explored and explained.

CONTRAST OF TIMBRE (antiphonal)

Antiphonal means "with contrasting voices" or "with contrast of timbre."

Contrast of timbre is keenest when presented with the surprises of sudden changes of tone color and register.

Antiphonal entrances can be made by a group of instruments, as in the first example, or in melodic form, as in the

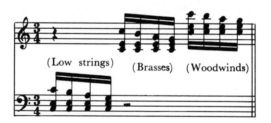

(Low strings)   (Brasses)   (Woodwinds)

or

(Clarinet)

(Violin)

second one. It is not necessary to change register as in the first example, but this is usually done. Note that the changes come rather rapidly and that there is recourse to the natural contrast in timbres between the instrumental families.

Occasionally the contrast will be applied more mildly, as in the next example, which features change of register within a family of instruments.

The antiphonal effect is most desirably stark when each new timbre can be heard without interference from any other element. Nevertheless, antiphonal alternation is also striking when acting in conjunction with another design element, as shown here:

Still another type of antiphonal interest is that which results when groups are placed off-stage in different parts of the auditorium and then are heard alternately as they answer back and forth. Good examples of this extraordinary effect are to be found in the use of offstage trumpet in the Beethoven *Leonore Overture No. 3* and in the Berlioz *Requiem*; the latter specifies performance with different groups stationed in various parts of the auditorium. The full excitement of such antiphonal music can be experienced only in actual performance.

Project 15

Write some examples which apply antiphonal techniques. Include both harmonic and melodic entrances and apply changes of register whenever possible.

At first, illustrate antiphonal contrast in its purest form, with the entering groups of voices sounding without interference from supplementary design. Later, apply it in combination with some simple supporting background. For instance, there could be woodwind melodies alternating antiphonally against a background of string harmony or antiphonal music for strings only, with the soloistic registers of viola and cello alternating melodically against a *pizzicato* background.

INSTRUMENTAL MOTION

Music may be defined as "sound in motion, within a span of time." There is a whole realm of meaning and poetic feeling in musical motion which stimulates a kinesthetic (motor) response. When an instrument is set into meaningful motion, an aura of attractiveness arises. A sudden flurry captures the attention, and any characterfully active design or live and continuous rhythmic pattern mysteriously magnifies the allure of a timbre.

The possibilities of instrumental motion are as rich and varied as are those of harmony or melody. These two facets have been carefully analyzed, but the processes and values of instrumental motion have remained largely untouched by practical analysis. Surely, here is an important theoretical frontier!

Although liveness of instrumental action was an important part of primitive music, its use diminished until Rimsky-Korsakov and others in the late nineteenth and early twentieth centuries brought about a revival of interest in kinesthetic values.

from BERLIOZ: *Symphonie fantastique* (Kalmus)

PLATE XVII. ANTIPHONAL CONTRAST

It is a special emphasis upon new frontiers in idiomatic invention that distinguishes modern from classic orchestration. Stravinsky is especially noteworthy for modern-day instrumental invention; Debussy and Rimsky-Korsakov were also very gifted in their motor sensibilities. Study some of the scores by these masters to analyze techniques of instrumental motion: for example, *La Mer* and *Ibéria* by Debussy, *Scheherazade* by Rimsky-Korsakov and *Petrouchka*, *Le Sacre du printemps* and *L'Histoire du soldat* by Stravinsky.

Project 16

After preliminary experimentation in invention of attention-getting motor activity for each instrument, use the best of the resulting measures as a basis from which to develop a number of short duos. Employ instruments which afford contrasting motor potentialities, such as fluidity opposed to brittleness (flute and wood block), *legato* opposed to *staccato* (saxophone and snare drum), substantiality opposed to delicacy (trumpet and *pizzicato* viola). If possible, include the piano or the harpsichord in some of the duo combinations, since these are natural instruments of motion. When instrumental motion is featured, the

from ROUSSEL: *The Spider's Feast* (Permission for reprint granted by Durand et Cie, Paris, France, copyright owners; Elkan-Vogel Co., Inc., Philadelphia, Pa., agents)

PLATE XVIII. INSTRUMENTAL MOTION

203

texture often will tend to be polythematic or polyrhythmic. There is an illustration of this type of combination on page 203.

DOUBLING FOR POWER

When two instruments are played in unison this is known as *doubling*. Indiscriminate doubling results in rather poor and characterless sound. A cardinal rule should be this:

Unless the purpose of the doubling is theoretically clear to the composer, he should avoid it.

There are only two good reasons for doubling: (1) for tonal power, and (2) for tonal subtlety. Even when consciously chosen, a doubling which continues for too long will become tiring to the ear. Use no doubling or unison blending except for definite dramatic, structural or coloristic purposes. Before scoring any doubling, justify its use by explaining to yourself why it is needed. If you cannot justify the doubling, use only the clear, unmixed tone color.

Acquaintance with scores will lead to the conclusion that some composers, such as Tchaikovsky, Mozart, Mendelssohn and Debussy, prefer the pure, unmixed tone colors. Others prefer the richness of blended tone. Beethoven uses a great deal of octave doubling; note that it is most often related to moments of power need. Rimsky-Korsakov does much melodic tone-mixing, and there are striking examples of blend for subtlety in Ravel's *Rapsodie espagnole*. The degree and type of doubling depend upon personal preference and artistic purpose.

The most common type of doubling is doubling for power. An intense and powerful sound results from multiple unison of timbres. This unison may be written either in a single line or in octaves. The more the doubling can be concentrated into one line (toward the middle register), the richer and more varied the effect will be. The more the octave doubling is utilized, the more powerful the effect will be.

(rich)   (strong)   (massive)

Project 17

Write examples which illustrate the three types of distribution shown just above: (a) actual unison, (b) unison with moderate octave doubling, and (c) unison with maximum octave doubling. As an exercise in transposition, score these illustrations of doubling with all parts correctly transposed.

Since the brass instruments tend to dominate, to become tiring, and do not have the natural agility of the woodwinds and strings, it is usually more effective in these unison passages for the brasses to sound only part of the time. This will make the impact of their power, when they do enter, much more fresh and telling (see p. 206).

This same limitation should be applied to the use of bell-toned percussion instruments (piano, xylophone, glockenspiel, etc.). In the orchestra their sounds are so attention-getting that the ear soon tires of them. This is also true of the piccolo. Such vivid timbres as these should be reserved for moments of surprise and brilliance and should be added to the unison only for a short spell.

A purely monophonic unison line is very effective, but it may be somewhat structurally dull. In many a score it will be

found that the structure has been livened by some small hetero-phonic enrichment or by a simple background. For example, to the above unison effect there might be added a simple reinforce-ment of the tonic center, to give a foundation or "floor" to the tonal structure—as in this example:

This music is still, in essence, doubling for power, even though a bit of additional structure has been supplied to keep it from being too spare. In fact, any effect is magnified by some slight supporting structure (like the setting around the diamond or the frame around the painting).

206

from TCHAIKOVSKY: *Romeo and Juliet* Overture (Bote and Bock)

PLATE XIX. DOUBLING FOR POWER

207

TIMBRE BLEND

The most subtle sounds result from the mixing of dissimilar timbres. A striking instance of the mixture of opposites is found in *Ibéria* by Debussy. At the beginning of the second movement, "Les Parfums de la nuit," Debussy blends the soft gentleness of the low register of the flute with the commonplace, solid "clink-clank" of the xylophone. The result is an unusual new sound, rich and alluring like a distant bell. Another striking instance of subtle blend is found in Tchaikovsky's *Romeo and Juliet* Overture, where viola and cor anglais are doubled in the famous melody. The blend of the mellowness of the viola tone with the "bite" and brooding "graininess" of the cor anglais tone, creates a sound of moving and memorable richness.

It seems that the most striking blends are derived from the combination of *only two* opposing timbres or, at most, the timbres of two contrasting melodic instruments combined with one dryer, percussive sound such as snare drum or *pizzicato* strings. When three or more sustained timbres are heard in unison, vividness of tonal character seems to merge into a general sound usually identified with reinforcement rather than subtlety.

The type of blend most often used for subtlety of sound is doubling which uses contrasting timbres sounding as a single line.

When a line is doubled with contrasting timbres an octave apart, there is less blend, but a striking freshness results.

from MCKAY: *Tlingit Suite*

When exact doubling is applied to choirs of contrasting timbre, the harmonic resonance has a less blended effect than that which results from a slight differentiation of action in the

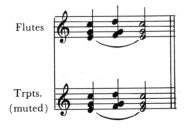

choirs (see the two examples above). Richard Wagner applied such a differentiation in his scoring. His main lines (main melody, bass line and counter melody) are doubled fully, but each supporting harmonic unit has its own independent design and spacing. This differentiation produces a delicately blended, yet not routinely exact mixing of resonances, which gives the impression that a superior type of tone-blending is being heard.

Earlier composers were not unaware of the possibilities of tone-blending. Bach used the plectrum sound of the harpsichord in his *concerti grossi*, and Renaissance composers often doubled vocal parts with orchestral instruments. In nineteenth-century music there was a tendency to use choirs of instruments of similar timbre, which caused some of the vitality of timbre to give way to harmonic values.

With the invention of new instruments in the twentieth century and the revival of some of the older ones, a new interest has developed in the many possibilities for timbre. Various mixed chamber-music combinations, and the chamber orchestra with one soloist on each instrument, are examples of instrumental groups which show a consciousness of new subtleties afforded by this increase in resources for diversified timbre.

Project 18

Write illustrations to show the use of timbre-mixing for subtlety. Write one example to illustrate melodic use, and another to illustrate the "Wagnerian" subtlety of harmonic effect (as shown in the examples on p. 210). Study the scores of the Prelude to *Tristan and Isolde* and the Prelude to *Lohengrin* by Wagner, to see how he has applied doubling to his melody (principally for strengthening) and subtle differentiation to the harmony.

From Wagner, *Tristan and Isolde*.

from DEBUSSY: *Ibéria* (Permission for reprint granted by Durand et Cie, Paris, France, copyright owners; Elkan-Vogel Co., Inc., Philadelphia, Pa., agents)

II._ Les parfums de la nuit

PLATE XX. BLEND FOR SUBTLETY

212

from RAVEL: *Rapsodie espagnole* (Permission for reprint granted by Durand et Cie, Paris, France, copyright owners; Elkan-Vogel Co., Inc., Philadelphia, Pa., agents) *III._ Habanera*

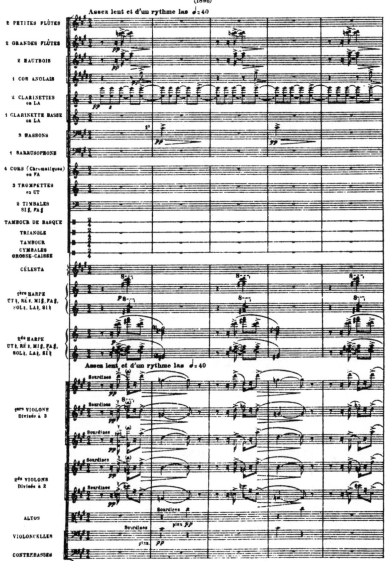

PLATE XXI. BLEND FOR SUBTLETY

CONTRAST OF PITCH LOCALE

Contrast between high and low pitch is a basic form of tonal interest. Extreme contrasts, such as piccolo and bass clarinet, produce a special bizarre effect:

Contrast of pitch can be applied antiphonally:

It can be used in simultaneous action as part of any textural type, as shown on the next page.

Project 19

Write examples using some contrast of high and low pitch. Write principal melodies and motives in extreme pitches. If any supplementary structure is added, place it in middle register to avoid interference with the main material.

from TCHAIKOVSKY: *Nutcracker Suite*

BLEND OF DIFFERENTIATED MOTION

If differing versions of a melody are played at the same time, or if a rhythm is diversified by the playing of one or more variants simultaneously, a special kind of tonal attractiveness is created. This attractiveness springs from a certain motor enrichment, a subtle complexity of seemingly simultaneous yet partially alternated activity.

215

from BERLIOZ: *Symphonie fantastique* (Kalmus)

PLATE XXII. CONTRAST OF PITCH LOCALE (high and low)

216

This heterophonic type of interest was common to primitive music and has become more and more a characteristic of twentieth-century orchestration. In the works of Debussy, Stravinsky, Martinu and others there is a subtle and glamorous quality to the motion that seems to come from elaborate design. In trying to equal this, the novice composer will often write a page with too many unrelated patterns of activity and motion. The elaboration in the music of the master composers is usually unified by the central force of principal rhythmic motives which have been expanded by simultaneous heterophonic variants.

To illustrate this procedure, a principal rhythmic motive is shown first in its elemental form, and then expanded into heterophonically elaborate complexity (opposite page).

Note that in the latter example the essentially rhythmic character of the principal motive has been retained in the variants to produce an over-all unity of rhythm. Although the second version is greatly diversified, it has the impact of a single unified action.

Project 20

Experiment separately with two types of heterophonic blend: (1) melodic, and (2) rhythmic. In accordance with the great central artistic principle of balancing complexity against simplicity, it is preferable that both melody and accompaniment not be complex at the same time. If the melody is heterophonically complex, keep the accompaniment simple (even sketchily delicate). Conversely, if the accompaniment is to be heterophonically elaborate, the melody should be stable and direct.

EXTREME REGISTERS

The interest created by use of extremes of register results from a certain stringency of timbre rather than from vividness

of pitch. The high register of the cello and the low register of the piccolo are really medium pitches, but both of these have unusual appeal because of the peculiarly individualistic and expressive timbre produced. Become acquainted with all the extreme high and low registers on the several instruments, such as the pedal-tone sound of the horn with its fantastic, subterranean excitement, the lyricism of the high tones of the tuba, and the "allure" of the flute in low register.

from MARTINU: *Sinfonia Concertante* (Copyright 1953 by B. Schott's Soehne, Mainz, by permission of the original copyright owner and its United States representative, Associated Music Publishers, Inc., New York)

PLATE XXIII. BLEND OF DIFFERENTIATED MOTION

219

The opening measures of *Le Sacre du printemps* by Stravinsky make extraordinary use of the extreme upper tones of the bassoon. *The Afternoon of a Faun* by Debussy begins with a flute solo in the exceedingly attractive lower register. In the first movement of *The Pines of Rome* Respighi achieves a stunning effect by piling up the intensity of many vivid instruments all sounding in high register.

In some of Debussy's music there is to be found a specialized use of non-extreme register. If all voices are restricted to use of the normal middle part of their ranges, an impression of delicacy, sweetness, and gentleness is effected.

Project 21

Listen to the qualities of the extreme registers of the instruments as played by individual instrumentalists, and to music by contemporary masters of orchestration who employ extreme registers. Make some use of these choice timbres in experiments of your own. Ordinarily the extremes of register will be used either for melody or for accompaniment, not for both. The object of experimentation for Project 21 will be to explore the use of clear unmixed tone color, rather than blend, which has been dealt with in Project 18.

CONTRASTED ARTICULATION

The drier percussion instruments like snare drum and wood block are stringent in their attack, and supply a harshness and vigor that is akin to dissonance. The plectrum (plucked) instruments (*pizzicato* strings, guitar, etc.) are pointed and immediate in articulation and supply a vigor of attack second only to the drier percussions. The strings when bowed produce a moderately stringent attack and can effect either *staccato* or *legato* with little

from STRAVINSKY: *Petrouchka* (Kalmus)

PLATE XXIV. EXTREME REGISTERS

effort. The brasses are instruments of sustained tone, but have some degree of articulative vigor. The bell-toned percussion instruments (glockenspiel, celesta, etc.) have a lesser degree of articulative vigor because of the softening effect of the harmonic (consonant) impression that they make. The woodwinds, especially the flutes, have the softest and gentlest articulation.

There are, therefore, six degrees of articulative intensity, ranging from harsh and vigorous to soft and gentle.

TABLE III

1.	Harsh and vigorous	(dry percussion)
2.	Pointed and vivid	(plectrum instruments)
3.	Moderately intense	(bowed strings)
4.	Less intense	(brass instruments)
5.	Softened by harmonic resonance	(bell-tone percussion)
6.	Soft and gentle	(woodwinds)

This scale of intensities leads to a formula for tonal interest:

The most striking blends of articulative types will result from combinations of the most extreme opposites.

Next in interest will be combinations of relatively opposite types. Least interesting will be combinations of the most nearly similar in articulative intensity.

Two examples of contrasted articulation are shown on page 223. (Flutes (blown) are mixed with celesta (percussive), and trombones (blown) are mixed with cymbals (struck). Both of these examples illustrate combination of articulative types.

It is in the music of the Orient that the most imaginative articulative resources can be found, particularly in the use of percussion instruments. Fascinating examples of mixture of articulative intensity may be heard in the Louisville recording *And the Fallen Petals*, by Chou Wen-Chung. In this work, by blending harsh percussive sounds with those of the blown instruments,

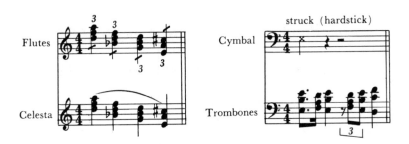

the composer has added an exciting dissonance to harmonies which, by themselves, are relatively consonant. Another good example of articulative mixture is the Louisville recording *Concerto No. 7* by Hovhaness, which brings in the bell sounds in an original way. "The Festival at Bagdad" from Rimsky-Korsakov's *Scheherazade*, and *The Fountains of Rome* by Respighi are also notable—the former for its vigorous combination of articulative types, and the latter for certain delectable blends (flute and harp, for instance).

Project 22

Experiment in the realm of articulative mixture. It will not be necessary to write full orchestral textures, since the knowledge about combinations could be tried out on a single melodic line. A single brass chord to which the roll of a snare drum is added offers a concentrated experience in the effects of articulative mixture. Try out many combinations in concentrated form.

OVERLAPPING

The tonal interest of overlapping stems from a type of "light and shade" which comes from alternation of blended and clear tone.

223

from RESPIGHI: *The Fountains of Rome* (By permission of G. Ricordi & Co., copyright owner)

PLATE XXV. CONTRASTED ARTICULATION (flute and harp)

The process may be symbolized by the following visual design:

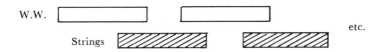

etc.

At first, only the woodwinds are heard. At another point, woodwinds and strings are heard together. At a third point, only the strings are sounding.

Project 23

In reduced scoring, invent some illustrations of overlapping: (a) between woodwind and string choirs, (b) between

225

the three choirs (woodwind, brass and strings), and (c) between two melodic voices over an accompaniment (homophonic texture). It is desirable to have interesting varieties in overlapping. That is, as in polyphony, the entrances must not be too monotonously regular or mechanical. The freedom and variety of the overlapping action of cloud forms, as they pass through the sky, will have an affinity to the values of overlapping in orchestration.

For practice in this technique it is best to use choirs of sound rather than single lines, although overlapping succeeds equally when applied to melodic lines. Study some of the examples of overlapping listed in the chart of examples for reference (see Table IX) in the Appendix on page 303).

Study as many other scores as you can, to find and analyze examples of overlapping. Ability to apply this principle should result from skill and insight acquired from ordinary contrapuntal studies. The scores of Sibelius, for example, show very little formal polyphony, but they have a wealth of the larger polyphony of overlapping (entrance and departure of the various choirs and design elements); this is an important element in any scoring.

POINTILLISM

Pointillism is a technique borrowed from the "Impressionistic" style of painting and transferred to music by Debussy and others. In such a painting, when seen from a distance, points of design seem to merge into a single impression; separated primary colors form an impression of a subtle blend.

To approximate this in music, a series of fragmentary designs must be sounded in clear timbres and in differing registers. Entrances should be heard only briefly and in rapid order. These splashes or points of sound are separated in space and time, but in the mind of the listener, they merge into an impression of blended tonal beauty. Analyze the use of this technique in

from BLACHER: *Studie im Pianissimo* (With authorization of Bote &
Bock, Berlin/Wiesbaden, Germany)

PLATE XXVI. OVERLAPPING

La Mer and *Ibéria* by Debussy. Successful pointillism demands a special clearness of timbre. Too much sustained sound should be avoided, but sometimes a very thin background of sustained motion may be added. This will give an underlying unity which will balance a certain "scrappiness" inherent in pointillism. This supplementary thread of motion must be subtle and delicate. A bit of overlapping in the pointillistic entrances helps give continuity to the sound, but is not essential. Observe these two "pointillistic" measures:

Project 24

Study Plate XXVI and the scores of Debussy for further illustration of "pointillistic" techniques. Write a page of score

which employs this technique. Use points of clear, unmixed tone color; have them enter rapidly and briefly. Locate each entry of new timbre in a non-competing pitch locale. Some supporting motion of a delicate continuing sort may be added. For this project it will be advisable to write in full score, since "pointillistic" tone-mixing demands such constant shifting to fresh tone color. It is best to have a large palette of orchestral color before the imagination, to ensure a variety of resources.

To supplement the study of Debussy scores, French impressionist paintings might also be studied and analyzed. This will heighten an understanding of the relationship of "pointillism" in orchestration to "pointillism" in painting.

TOTAL MIXTURE

There has already been a discussion of mixture by doubling (p. 204). Mixture without doubling has a significantly different, more rarefied sound which results from clear points of tone color sounding simultaneously in separate designs and pitch locales. Theoretically, all the basic tonal ingredients, if heard in a maximum combination, should produce a blend which is uniquely rich and full.

There are eight basic tonal ingredients. An objectively calculated total mixture would include the following types:

TABLE IV

1. "Soft" woodwinds	(flutes and clarinets)
2. "Harsh" woodwinds	(oboes and bassoons)
3. "Warm" brass	(horns and muted brasses)
4. "Clear" brass	(trumpets, trombones)
5. The string tone	(violins, violas, cellos)
6. Plectrum sounds	(harp, harpsichord, guitar, *pizzicato* strings)
7. Bell-tone percussion	(piano, celesta, etc.)
8. "Dry" percussion	(snare drum, woodblock, tambourine, etc.)

from RAVEL: *Rapsodie espagnole* (Permission for reprint granted by Durand et Cie, Paris, France, copyright owners; Elkan-Vogel Co., Inc., Philadelphia, Pa., agents)

PLATE XXVII. POINTILLISM

The most complete small instrumental group would, therefore, include one player for each of the above timbres.

Through small combinations, which can include unusual bell-tone and plectrum instruments such as vibraphone and guitar, certain orchestrators—following in the footsteps of Webern—seem to be striving toward an ideal of total mixture. The smallness of the groups used ensures vividness, while the addition of unusual instruments adds vigor and allure through variety and contrast.

All eight basic ingredients will not necessarily be present in the instrumentation of such small groups, but the tendency is toward completeness through the use of the contrast potentialities latent in the eight basic categories. How complete would a combination of xylophone, harpsichord, flute, viola, snare drum and contralto voice be? How complete would a combination of accordion, guitar, trombone and double bass be? Try to think of several such ensemble combinations with relative completeness of mixture in mind.

Project 25

To experiment with the effect of total mixture, choose one instrument from each of the eight categories listed above. Write a piece (a few measures) in which, at some point, all eight basic types of timbre are sounding simultaneously, as in the example on page 232. Listen to *Le Marteau sans maître* by Boulez, and to the complete works of Webern (recorded by Robert Craft). Also compare the instrumentation of various modern dance bands and other small combinations, in order to make objective theoretical judgments as to their relative degrees of "total mixture."

Britten's *Serenade for Tenor, Horn and Strings*, Varèse's *Octandre* and the symphonies of Milhaud are valuable for such analytical comparison.

It is interesting to observe how certain ingredients of "total mixture" have come into and gone out of fashion. Plectrum in-

Category

struments such as lutes and mandolins, now seldom used, were an important part of early Italian orchestras. The harpsichord was very prominent in the time of Bach, but practically disappeared until revived in the twentieth century. The *Petite Symphonie Concertante* by Frank Martin, which features harp, harpsichord and piano in combination with strings, is typical of the revived twentieth-century interest in plectrum sound.

Handel's *Water Music* was played on a barge floating down the Thames. The orchestra was made up of oboes, bassoons and strings, a jolly but incomplete instrumentation. In the Classical Period, there was almost an over-emphasis on the strings. In America, in the early twentieth century, the strings almost withered away and disappeared from dance bands. The symphonic band has shown a one-sided over-emphasis on the clarinet and brass sounds.

CONTRAST OF CHORD AND LINE

When a melodic line cuts through a mass of sound, the contrast which is effected has inherent tonal interest. The usual homophonic manifestation of melody and accompaniment is a contrast of chord and line, but its choicest sound comes from the subtle tone-mixing that results when the line cuts through a chordal structure which is in a similar pitch locale. This brings about a blend of tone and action that can be derived in no other way.

The *Midsummer Night's Dream* Overture of Mendelssohn (shown in the first two examples on p. 236) shows considerable use of this principle, as does the *Tannhäuser* excerpt of Wagner (shown in the third example). The result in each case is a strangely appealing warmth and richness. Analyze the examples on p. 236.

from MARTIN: *Petite Symphonie Concertante* (Universal Edition, copyright owner; permission for reprint granted by Theodore Presser Company, representative for the U.S.A., Canada and Mexico)

PLATE XXVIII. UNUSUAL INSTRUMENTATION

from WEBERN: *Fünf geistliche Lieder* (Universal Edition, copyright owner; permission for reprint granted by Theodore Presser Company, representative for the U.S.A., Canada and Mexico.

[Doppelcanon in motu contrario]

PLATE XXIX. TOWARD TOTAL MIXTURE (vertical)

235

Project 26

In reduced scoring, invent some examples of chord contrasting with line. Use contrasting timbres in similar registers: e.g., string harmony, with *cor anglais* in a line cutting through it; or woodwinds in harmony, with a violin line cutting through (sounding in the same pitch locale).

Oboe

Strings

* point of dissonance

The above example shows how dissonance can be absorbed and softened by contrast of timbre and contrast of chord and line. Try this out.

MOTION AS A SUSTAINING FACTOR

When Sibelius said, "The orchestra has no pedal," he meant: if you want the sound in the orchestra to ring the way it does on the piano, you will have to add sustaining tones or choirs to the scoring. When Wagner said, "The secret of good orchestral sound is sustained tone," he had the same general problem in mind.

Unsustained, fragmented or "pointillistic" sound tends to "dry out" and apparently to lack a "floor" or "foundation." It is true that the addition of too much sustaining sound tends to

237

from FRANCK: *Symphony in D minor* (Kalmus)

PLATE XXX. CONTRAST OF CHORD AND LINE

obscure delicacy of design, but there is a way to achieve foundational feeling without adding actual sustaining material. This can be done through the use of some simple continuous motion pattern: for example,

If there is some stabilizing motion of this kind in the score, the rest of the music may be very "fragmentary" or "pointillistic," and it will still seem satisfyingly unified. Without this thread of motion there might be a feeling of breathlessness and uncertainty.

The line of motion may be in any pitch locale, but should remain thin and delicate (a unit of one or two voices only).

Respighi makes effective use of this principle in *The Fountains of Rome*.

This principle is still another representation of contrast in action—fragmentariness contrasted to stability and steadiness (as shown opposite).

Without the stabilizing action of the violas, the sound would be very fragmentary.

Project 27

Experiment with the balancing of fragmentariness against a thin line of continuous motion, as in the following example.

239

PERCUSSION AS BACKGROUND

Because of its aural vividness, the pulsating timbre of a percussive element can supply a stabilizing effect. The striking sound and penetrating force of percussion rhythm so engages the attention and so definitely—and almost hypnotically—fills up the sound space that everything else seems almost incidental. If a drum beat such as the following is begun,

even random shouts and noises, if added, seem to merge into meaning, through the unifying power and dominating energy and impact of such a motor pedal (rhythmic *ostinato*).

from RESPIGHI: *The Fountains of Rome* (© 1918 by G. Ricordi & Co., Milan. Reprinted by permission.)

PLATE XXXI. MOTION AS A SUSTAINING FACTOR

Primitive peoples knew about this principle, and used drums in this way as a strong unifying force. Jazz musicians understand its power, and use percussion as a foundation for improvisatory freedom. Much tonal interest results from the variety of timbre made possible by the unifying percussive background.

Project 28

On any vivid percussion instrument, start a "beat," or rhythmic pattern, and then add any random or fragmentary material. Use only small combinations, as in this example, and write several short examples of your own.

STRINGS AS BACKGROUND

Throughout the Classic and Romantic Periods, the strings were used as the mainstay of orchestral sound. The woodwinds were secondary in importance and often doubled or reinforced the strings, while the brass and percussion were used as supporting strength on *forte* passages. Mozart and von Weber began to break through its limited use, but it was only in the Debussy "impressionistic" style and after invention of certain mechanical improvements (Boehm system fingerings for the woodwinds and valve systems for the brasses) that a more developed use of brass and woodwinds began.

242

from VILLA-LOBOS: *Chôros No. 10*, "Rasga o Coração" (Copyright 1928, by Editions Max Eschig, Paris. Copyright renewed 1956. Used by permission of the original copyright owners and their United States representative, Associated Music Publishers, Inc., New York)

PLATE XXXII. PERCUSSION AS BACKGROUND

As the woodwinds and brasses became more soloistic and individually capable, the roles of the instruments were reversed. The strings became background (they can, indeed, make a wonderful background) and the brasses and woodwinds (particularly the woodwinds) became foreground. As will be explained later, this use of the woodwinds as foreground, with strings as background, is a more nearly natural balance of the idiomatic characteristics of the choirs.

Debussy nearly always included the harp in his orchestrating; and Manuel de Falla included the piano to make a more complete balance of character in the sound, and to approach the "total mixture" (non-doubled) already discussed.

String sound can be so delicate and varied that the invention of string patterns for background has endless and fascinating possibilities. As this naturally fluent, vague and active background material combines with a foreground of definite woodwind and brass timbres, there is a new liveness and attractiveness of sound in the whole orchestra.

Listen, with score in hand, first to a classic work and then to a Debussy work, in which strings recede to the background and woodwinds take over the foreground. The live and luminous quality of the Debussy score will be immediately apparent.

Study many contemporary scores to analyze the techniques that produce this special type of tonal interest, to see how subsequent composers have utilized the ideas explored and revealed by Debussy. Scores especially recommended for this are *La Mer* and *Ibéria* by Debussy, *Escales* by Ibert, the *Daphnis and Chloé* Suites by Ravel, and *Trois Poèmes Juifs* by Bloch.

Project 29

Invent a background of string motion, using the entire string section; then add woodwind and brass melodies, as in the following illustration:

PUNCTUATION

An accented point or important entrance can be intensified or highlighted by reinforcing it briefly with additional design. This will be referred to as *punctuation*. This effect is somewhat related to the heterophonic unison, but is more briefly applied, and the punctuating factor has little consecutive meaning. The point of punctuation is merely a touch of emphasis, but the tonal effect gives extra strength and variety to an orchestral idea.

245

from SCHUMANN: *Symphony No. 1 in B-flat Major,* "Spring" (Kalmus)

PLATE XXXIII. STRINGS AS BACKGROUND

Striking suddenness can bring a feeling of pleasant surprise. The two examples below show this principle in action.

Project 30

Search in various scores for illustrations of punctuation; then write some examples of your own. See the novel use of flutes for punctuation at the very opening of *L'Apprenti sorcier* by Dukas; the single explosive chord at the beginning of "Ronde du Sabbat" from *Symphonie fantastique* by Berlioz; and the woodwind *sforzando* effect at measure 297 in the *Symphony No. 8* by Beethoven. It will take some searching to find other examples, but almost any well-written score will make some use of this principle.

from GUARNIERI: *Prologo e Fuga* (Copyright 1951 by Associated Music Publishers, Inc., New York—used by permission)

PLATE XXXIV. PUNCTUATION

BALANCE OF IDIOMATIC CHARACTERISTICS

Each family of instruments has a particular kinesthetic personality. The brasses are slower in articulation and are naturally harmonic. The woodwinds are more moderate in speed and tend naturally toward melody. The strings are accurate and rapid in articulation and are well suited to florid design.

If this comparison is followed through, it will lead to the conclusion that there is a normal "good sound" which results when these three main families of instruments are used together, fulfilling their naturally supplementary and somewhat contrasting kinesthetic roles (woodwind melodic—brass sustaining—strings in active design). This "good sound" can be said to result from simultaneous fulfillment of natural "roles" or, in other words, from a *balance of idiomatic characteristics*.

For special effects this normal interplay of kinesthetic qualities may be reversed. The brass might become melodic, the strings harmonic and slow-moving, and the woodwinds agile and decorative. The effect would be striking, as are all intentional distortions and grotesques.

Composers differ considerably in their uses of this principle of balance. Sibelius, for instance, uses a normal balance of articulative speed and makes much of it. Hindemith, on the other hand, prefers to have the instruments on an equal footing much of the time, with all instruments busy, in a sort of musical democracy. In one sense, this is musically progressive and tends to liberate and develop the slower-moving instruments into more challenging activity; but it also loses the simple strength of normal balance. The following excerpt from Beethoven's *Symphony No. 6* shows an old-fashioned, but healthy, balance of articulation and motion. Note that the strings are active, the woodwinds moderate in speed, and the brass slow and sustaining.

249

Project 31

Write pages of full score which begin by illustrating the normal balance of idiomatic characteristics. On the first page exemplify ordinary balance, as in the Beethoven example shown above; then try out some variation of the normal balance with strings sustaining, and the brass active; or with the brass moderately active and melodic, while woodwinds are active.

CONTRAST OF STACCATO AND LEGATO (consecutive)

All effective phrasing, bowing or shaping of ideas will make some use of contrast of *staccato* and *legato* in consecutive action. To illustrate this, an ordinary scale passage will do.

Sawed out by the violins in this expressionless *détaché* bowing, the result is quite dull:

Almost equally dull is this version, in which there is a uniformly smooth and eventless *legato*:

How much more character even an ordinary scale takes on when *staccato* and *legato* contrast is added to its shaping!

from DVOŘÁK: *Symphony No. 8 in G Major* (Novello)

PLATE XXXV. BALANCE OF IDIOMATIC CHARACTERISTICS

from MENDELSSOHN: *The Hebrides Overture* (Kalmus)

PLATE XXXVI. BALANCE OF IDIOMATIC CHARACTERISTICS

This inner contrast within a line is one way to create enjoyable sound; all successful composers make use of it. Haydn, in particular, was especially creative with this process, and all the composers of the Classic Period made much of this "architectural" contrast. Contrast of *staccato* and *legato* is particularly necessary in the writing of string parts. With the many alternatives of bowing available, there are wonderfully rich possibilities for invention in the shaping of string design. Study the classic string quartets to get a feeling for subtleties of bowing. Observe the *staccato* and *legato* design in this excerpt from Beethoven's *Symphony No. 6*:

Project 32

Invent a page of score in which contrast of *staccato* and *legato* is applied to melodic line. Also write any number of unison or single lines featuring *staccato* and *legato* in contrast.

STACCATO AND LEGATO (simultaneous)

Nothing sounds more live and interesting than a musical structure in which continuous *staccato* and continuous *legato* sound simultaneously, as in this excerpt from Brahms's *Piano Concerto No. 2*:

The scores of Saint-Saëns are particularly vivid in their use of this principle. Composers vary in their uses of *staccato* and *legato*. Some, like Franck, Delius, and Wagner, tend to be somewhat monotonously *legato*; whereas others, like Scarlatti and Prokofiev, are more *staccato*. The ideal or norm should be a balance of *staccato* and *legato* and sufficient use of the simultaneous contrast, as in the above example.

Project 33

Invent some structures using simultaneous *staccato* and *legato*. Keep in mind that the individual lines need not be as

from MOZART: *Symphony No. 25 in G minor*, K. 183 (Heugel & Cie, Editeurs, Paris, copyright owner; permission for reprint granted by Theodore Presser Company, representative for the U.S.A., Canada and Mexico)

PLATE XXXVII. *Staccato* AND *Legato* IN CONTRAST (consecutive)

thematically important as are the two themes in the above example. In a homophonic texture, the accompaniment could be quite subordinate, and still supply a very vital *staccato* element against a *legato* melody; or there could be a *legato* accompaniment against a *staccato* melody.

EXPANDED TONAL GROUPS

The rich full-sounding harmonies of Wagner and other late-Romantic composers brought about an expansion in orchestral instrumentation. To the wind choirs, new and deeper timbres were added; the strings were often divided and the number of voices multiplied in both high and low registers.

To the woodwind section Wagner added a third flute, the cor anglais, bass clarinet, and a third bassoon. Each woodwind timbre could then have its own independent three-part harmony, as shown below. This created a new depth and richness in the

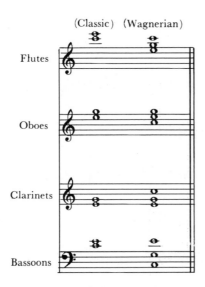

257

CREATIVE ORCHESTRATION

from SAINT-SAËNS: *Danse macabre* (Kalmus)

PLATE XXXVIII. *Staccato* AND *Legato* IN CONTRAST (simultaneous)

woodwind choir. Villa-Lobos and others have occasionally added saxophones for even further deepening.

It was in scoring for the string section that the most significant expansion took place; here, again, Wagner was an important innovator. The string unit in the classic orchestra was essentially like a string quartet, but with a little extra strength in the center and with the cello doubled by bass (sounding an octave lower). Wagner at times wrote for an ensemble in which each string timbre sounded as an independent choir—as shown here:

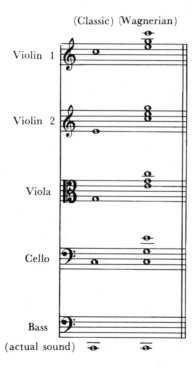

259

There are a great many possibilities for spacing such *divisi* strings. It is largely a matter of personal choice and dramatic fitness, but each harmonic grouping must have structural and harmonic consistency. Wagner's *Lohengrin* Prelude shows a highly effective use of divided strings; so does *The Swan of Tuonela* by Sibelius. Another major work for strings is *Fantasia on a Theme by Thomas Tallis* by Vaughan Williams, which employs two string orchestras and a string quartet to create unusual variety in string writing. Still another outstanding work of this type is the *Concerto for Two String Orchestras* by Martinu.

Divided strings produce an enjoyable full and creatively expressive tone quality. A significant enrichment takes place from the strengthened lower registers. On the other hand, when the higher strings are divided without the foundation of the lower string tone they become particularly "etherealized," as in the opening of the famous *Lohengrin* Prelude.

While there were important additions to the woodwind choir and expansions in the string choir during the Wagnerian period, the groupings in the brass section showed less change.

The band profits from the use of flügelhorns because of the more truly deep trumpet sound; but, as a general rule, the piling up of brass timbres too often results in a heavy, qualitatively inferior sound. The power of the brass is so striking that two trumpets and one trombone can create the illusion of a multitude and "blow down the walls of Jericho" without further aid. For this reason the brass choir has not often been expanded.

The baritone horn, or tenor tuba, is an unusual brass instrument which is sometimes added. For an illustration of expanded brass section, study the final movement of *The Pines of Rome* by Respighi. For an example of the use of both cornets and trumpets in the brass section, study the Franck *Symphony in D minor*. For illustration of the use of baritone horn, examine *The Planets* ("Mars") by Holst and the arrangement of *When Johnny Comes Marching Home* by Roy Harris.

The tuba must be used sparingly. It is most valuable for doubling of the lower trombone part when deep power is needed, but it is inevitably slow in articulation, and its too constant use will tend to retard action and blur sonority.

Project 34

The most effective exercise in the use of an expanded choir will come from writing small compositions for: (1) the full woodwind choir, (2) the full brass choir, and (3) the string orchestra. For the woodwind group use the full-fledged Wagnerian or "modern orchestra" woodwinds, with the inclusion of third flute, cor anglais, bass clarinet and third bassoon. Add any saxophones that you need for experiment. Use the chordal texture for these expanded unit exercises, as this will supply additional concentrated practice in organizing for unit consistency.

In the brass example use the standard "modern orchestra" grouping—four horns, three trumpets, three trombones and tuba. Add baritone horns if you wish. Here again, use a texture which is "chordal" in type. This will give additional experience in spacing and unit organization.

For the string ensemble use the string section of the standard symphony orchestra—first violins, second violins, viole, celli and bassi. Experiment with some divisi multiplication of parts. Because the strings have so many possibilities of distribution, more textural variety and imagination will be in order.

Any of the separate timbres of the string group may be expanded into independent choirs (first violins, second violins, viole or celli). Or some may be harmonic groups while others are not. This gives the orchestrator much more freedom of choice.

The basses are usually used for doubling of the bass line, but in rare instances have also been used for harmonic choirs.

Such bass harmonies have usually been scored to sound separately, so that their rather delicate timbre will not be obscured.

261

from R. STRAUSS: *Till Eulenspiegels lustige Streiche* (Kalmus)

PLATE XXXIX. EXPANDED WOODWIND SECTION

from SIBELIUS: *The Swan of Tuonela* (Kalmus)

PLATE XL. EXPANDED STRING SECTION

FRONTIERS

In the future the fundamental need for new tonal interest will continue to stimulate a search for new resources in timbre differentiation. The tendency toward expanded units, explored in Project 34, is only one of the "frontiers" of tonal interest. Other newer techniques still in early stages of exploration are: fuller and more subtle use of percussion instruments; total mixture (horizontal); total mixture (vertical); "music concrete"; electronic music, and the addition of human voices, as wordless timbres, to the orchestral sound. Every young musician will certainly want to explore these developing areas.

There is some possibility that these new resources are partially overrated, and that they may turn out to be not "revolutionary" but only "evolutionary." The various new effects and resources may not replace the effects of the traditional orchestra, but may only merge into a total technique, with all the established instruments still playing their fundamental and nourishing roles.

Nevertheless, the composers who have been most strikingly inventive and who have therefore dominated the realm of famous orchestrators are those like Berlioz, Wagner and Debussy, who kept abreast of mechanical improvements and opportunities and turned them into musical magic. Beethoven, in his day, also drove players to new levels of technical skill by demanding increased independence of each instrument and by writing works of more technical difficulty.

Project 35

Although no specific technical projects are offered, it is recommended that the study of orchestration include experimentation in these several "frontier" areas. If electronic devices are not available, young composers might band together to procure equipment and initiate joint experimental projects.

264

THE FULL AND SUBTLE USE OF PERCUSSION INSTRUMENTS

Although for centuries the music of primitive, ancient and oriental peoples had a highly developed art of percussion, the familiar European orchestral music has been somewhat under-developed in its use of percussive timbre. At some point in history European composers began to introduce certain Turkish military instruments into their music to simulate the exotic. The habit became established in bands and orchestras without being fully understood or explained—a striking example of "cultural lag" for the sociologist to consider.

A commonplace set of sounds—the snare drum, bass drum, cymbal and timpani—continues to dominate our music. One of the saddest of this writer's memories is the performance of *Londonderry Air* by a high school band, with the full percussion section idiotically playing along with the familiar "chunk-a-chunk" of the military instruments, almost completely negating the poetry of this beautiful folk song.

Carlos Chávez and others have made use of unusual native Latin-American percussion (e.g., *Sinfonia India*), and certain "avant-garde" composers, notably Cage, have made use of various unheard-of combinations with emphasis on the shockingly un-orthodox ("lion's roar," "typewriters," "tin pans," etc.) What the art of percussion still lacks is a sufficient scientific analysis of the potentialities of percussion timbres and a systematic categoriza-tion which will make available to the composer a much wider choice of percussion types. The future will also certainly bring into our music the already established and extraordinarily varied and subtle timbres of Asian and African musical traditions.

There is a most valuable section in the *Thesaurus of Orchestral Devices* by Gardner Read, in which he has listed the many subtle ways of treating the familiar percussion instruments.

This book includes references to specific measures in many scores where particular usages can be found. Complete knowledge and experimentation should eventually "cure" Western music of its too frequent addiction to the Turkish military instruments and too many mere "noise makers," such as the rattle, the whistle, the whip, and other approximations of "everydayness." The University of California at Los Angeles and The University of Washington have instituted special courses in the techniques of oriental music, and there are other evidences that music is nearing a "break-through" into a new and experimentally vital attitude toward idiophonic values.

TOTAL MIXTURE (horizontal)

This terminology best describes a technique applied by Anton von Webern in orchestration. If a given line maintains a tone color only briefly, and kaleidoscopically changes from one timbre to another, a horizontally applied total mixture is effected. This is a rarely used technique, rich in possibility. In the Columbia recording of Webern's complete works there is an example of this technique in his orchestration of a Bach fugue—listen to this recording. The ordinary orchestrator would have shown a tendency to follow through with the same tone color throughout a given segment of melody, but Webern changes the melodic timbre frequently and rapidly. The result is a sound that possibly violates the sturdy spirit of the music of Bach, but no one can deny the richness and tonal interest of this variegation, or fail to note that it is of "frontier" significance.

In a much more expansive way *Concerto for Orchestra* by Bartók sets out to ensure that all the instruments of the orchestra will be heard in turn as melodic voices. Over a very large span, this achieves a similar total mixture.

266

from MILHAUD: *Les Choéphores* (Copyright by Heugel, 1926–1947, Heugel, Editeur, Paris; permission for reprint granted by Theodore Presser Company, representative for the U.S.A., Canada and Mexico)

PLATE XLI. FULL AND SUBTLE USE OF PERCUSSION INSTRUMENTS

267

TOTAL MIXTURE (vertical)

This has already been discussed as a principle of tonal interest (total mixture non-doubled) but it also needs to be emphasized as a "frontier" potentiality. Webern is also an innovator in the use of this technique, and his orchestral pieces should be studied as illustrations of total mixture, along with those of Boulez and other twentieth-century French composers. Mention must also be made of the way in which the American jazz movement is similarly, but rather gropingly, reaching out in this direction by exploiting a great variety of small combinations.

"MUSIC CONCRETE"

The term *music concrete* refers to a music which makes use of sounds recorded from nature—bird calls, waterfalls, car brakes screeching, water gurgling out of a bottle, etc. These sounds are transformed by tape recorder techniques. New effects are created by transposing realistic sounds to higher and lower octaves. This distortion, by slowing down and speeding up the vibration, results in a new, sometimes sensational and grotesque tonal character. The Louisville recording *Music for Tape Recorder and Orchestra*, by Ussachevsky and Luening, is an attempt to reach out in this direction.

ELECTRONIC MUSIC

This is machine-produced music, with the tones played and created by electronic devices. Electronic music, as composed by Stockhausen and others, envisions a music which is no longer limited to the tonal systems of the various instruments. Such a music explores a world of sounds and timbres no longer limited by human inabilities. Almost any rhythm, any pitch, or any

268

timbre that can be scientifically calculated can be manufactured by combining various frequencies. Sound and motion will be completely freed from the human limitations of the orchestra player.

This revolutionary possibility will be deplored and combatted by those who treasure "humanism" in its old-fashioned sense, but it will be welcomed by those who see in it a new "humanism" in terms of the expressive possibilities of the controlled machine. Here, again, is a grand hope which may eventually be only partially realized. Perhaps electronic timbres will merely merge with already established sounds, to make a newly enriched total orchestral art. As mankind entered the age of science, it was natural that the artists and theorists should try to create new tonal types by scientific and mechanical means. For a time, around 1920 to 1930, there was much experimentation with such things as electrically produced tone, scratchings on the sound track, aluminum violins, glass clarinets, the Theremin, the Ondes Martenot, and the Hammond organ.

At this time there was great machine-age hopefulness that a whole new world of timbre would arise from new inventions such as these. Some of these temporarily exciting and unusual sounds were tentatively used for dramatic purposes, and serious composers began to be interested in them. These inventions and experimental sounds failed, however, to make a very lasting impression. Why was this? A comparison of basic timbres with the primary colors will help to explain this relative failure.

In visual experience, we are familiar with the seven colors contained in the rainbow (violet, indigo, blue, green, yellow, orange, red). Other colors, however marvelous and subtle they may be, are merely combinations of these. In the world of sound, there seem to be timbres which are similarly basic. These have been chosen as archetypes after centuries of musical evolution. The flute, the oboe, the horn, the trumpet, the harp, etc., are basic types of timbre so positively selected by the ear from hundreds of early timbre types that any tonal effect or combination of tone, or newly invented device, will inevitably sound like a mixture of these prototypical timbres. The Theremin and other electrical instruments sound like odd, imperfect flutes, while the Hammond organ too often sounds like a generalized mixture of strings and oboe. The saxophone is an interesting case in point: it disappears into the ensemble sound because it is neither a brass nor a woodwind but a relatively bland mixture of the two.

It would be no surprise to find that all future inventions of timbre must inevitably refer back to the present ones for qualitative definition, just as all colors must refer back to the spectrum. Nevertheless, as more analytical experimentation takes place and as psychological knowledge about "attributes" of tone becomes firmer, there will be constant attempts to invent new sounds and tonal devices.

Successful use of electronic devices can be heard in *Turangalila* by Messiaen, *Poème Electronique* and *Deserts* by Varèse and *Differences* by Berio. The latter can be especially commended for opening up new frontiers in application of sterophonic listening and for a more musically gifted treatment of timbre and motion that are typically electronic.

ORCHESTRAL USE OF HUMAN VOICES

In his *Three Nocturnes*, Debussy adds a choir of feminine voices to the instruments of the orchestra. In the movement "Sirènes" they sing harmonically as though they were a choir of instruments but use only syllables such as "ah," "la," etc. Holst in *The Planets* ("Neptune") makes similar harmonic use of human voices. Vaughan Williams uses the human voice as a solo instrument in the *Pastoral Symphony* and uses choral sound instrumentally in *Flos Campi*.

EDGARD-VARESE   DESERTS

INSTRUMENTATION

2 Flutes (Alt. Piccs.)
2 Clarinets in Bb (one Alt. Eb Cl., one Alt. Bass-Cl.)
2 Horns
3 Trumpets
    1st in D
    2nd and 3rd in C
3 Trombones
 Bass Tuba
 Contra-Bass Tuba
 Piano

Percussion:

I.   4 Timpani (with pedals) — Vibraphone — 2 Suspended Cymbals (high and low) –- Side Drum — Claves

II. Glockenspiel — Snare Drum — Field Drum — Side Drum — 2 Timbales or Tom-toms — 2 Suspended Cymbals (high and low) — Cencerro — Tambourine — (take Chinese Blocks from V. at Bar 200)

III. 2 Bass Drums (medium and low) with Attached Cymbals — Field Drum — Side Drum — Cencerro — Guiro — Claves — Tambourine — Chimes (Tubular Bells)

IV. Vibraphone — 3 Gongs (high, medium and low) — 2 Lathes — Guiro — Tambourine

V. Xylophone — 3 Chinese Blocks — 3 Wooden Drums (Dragon Heads) — Guiro — Claves — 2 Maracas — (take 2 Lathes from IV. at Bar 135)

2 Magnetic Tapes of electronically organized sounds transmitted on 2 channels by means of a stereophonic system.

The instruments and the interpolations of organized sound are never heard simultaneously, but must follow each other without a break, alternating as follows:

1. Instruments — from beginning to bar 82

2. 1st interpolation of organized sound enters on 4th beat of bar 82

3. Instruments enter bar 83 (¾ = ♩ = 100)

4. 2nd interpolation of organized sound enters on 2nd beat of bar 224

5. Instruments enter bar 225 (7/4 = ♩ = 132)

6. 3rd interpolation of organized sound enters on 4th beat of bar 263

7. Instruments enter bar 264 (5/4 = ♩ = 84)

The engineer at the magnetophone will signal the conductor for entrance of instruments.

This work may also be performed instrumentally without the interpolations of the tapes (electronically organized sound) if these are not available.

PLATE XLII. INSTRUCTIONS FOR THE USE OF ELECTRONICALLY PRODUCED SOUNDS from RAVEL: *Daphnis et Chloé* (Permission for reprint granted by Durand et Cie, Paris, France, copyright owners; Elkan-Vogel Co., Inc., Philadelphia, Pa., agents)

PLATE XLIII. ORCHESTRAL USE OF HUMAN VOICES

from SCHÖNBERG: *Pierrot Lunaire* (Used by permission of Belmont Music Publishers, Los Angeles, California, and Universal Edition, Vienna. Copyright 1956 by Gertrud Schoenberg)

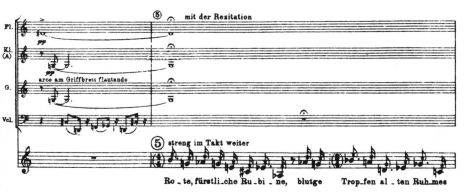

PLATE XLIV. SMALL EXPERIMENTAL COMBINATION

273

Theoretical analysis of the characteristics of vocal timbre might lead to the conclusion that voices are not really suitable as orchestral ingredients, if judged by what they add to the concept of "total mixture." Nevertheless, there are interesting frontiers in the possibilities for combining orchestral and vocal timbres.

Project 35

Write at least one example which explores a "frontier" area.

Have open-mindedness toward all new possibilities, but at the same time keep alive an understanding of fundamental values. Stravinsky, in his *Six Lessons in the Poetics of Music*, defines tradition as that which still succeeds in bringing forth the miracle of artistic value. All of the principles of clarity and tonal interest will still "work" as long as man is psychologically the creature that he is. However, language always grows and, since musical expression is also a "language," it will similarly grow throughout the future, as new sounds and new ways of producing them are constantly sought.

4

Structural
Values

*I*N ADDITION TO CLARITY AND TONAL EXCITEMENT, THE
best orchestration will also have effective structural design. Since structure is so organically related to musical form
and techniques of composition, a complete analysis of what
makes appealing structure would require a separate treatise.
Nevertheless, it is important to consider a few of the larger
generalizations that underlie such a complete analysis.

Fundamental sources of imaginative structure are: (a) sufficient instrumental motion; (b) sufficient vigor of design; (c)
sufficient overlapping of choirs; (d) "light and shade" through
variegation of "thickness and thinness" of texture, and (e) sufficient variety within general design.

SUFFICIENT INSTRUMENTAL MOTION

The structural vividness or challenge of orchestration will
depend greatly upon the ability of the composer to invent instrumental motion which is appealingly alive and natural to each
instrument. Simple motion can be characterful, but even within
a simple action there must be a purposeful design and a sense

of latent spontaneity. In scores which manifest elaborate motion there is nearly always a simple inner design which is the real unifying force. The score of Ravel's *Daphnis et Chloé* (Suite No. 2) is an illustration of this. At first glance there seems to be unparalleled elaboration; but upon further analysis it can be seen that the elaboration coalesces into unified main streams of tonal action which are essentially simple, in spite of all the apparent surface "busyness."

SUFFICIENT VIGOR OF DESIGN

The value of sufficient design is illustrated in the following three examples:

Here the viola design is rather blank and has almost no significant structure. If a mere grace note is added to the viola part, as in the next example, the design is strengthened and made more tangible, and the musical feeling immediately becomes heightened.

If the viola part is further strengthened by more definite design, as shown below, the result will be even more striking.

SUFFICIENT OVERLAPPING OF CHOIRS

If the entrance of the choirs (woodwind, brass and strings) is merely antiphonal, or if the choirs constantly enter together, the result may be somewhat crude or monotonous. Such primitively simple unity of action can be used intentionally with strong and purposeful effect. However, most of the time there must be an essentially polyphonic plasticity of choir action derived from overlapping.

There is always a need for open space in any musical design, and this can be effected by the entry and departure of choirs from the fabric of sound. Such "sculptured silence" gives the mind of the listener more time to fasten upon the tangibilities of motive and pattern. Also, pauses for breath are always desirable for the various players.

"LIGHT AND SHADE" THROUGH VARIEGATION OF "THICKNESS AND THINNESS" OF TEXTURE

Thickness or thinness can be regulated and varied by increasing or reducing the number of voices. A too thin scoring, too long continued, becomes disappointing. A scoring with too many voices, too long continued, becomes wearing. Structural eventfulness is dependent upon a balance between these two extremes. Such a variegation of thickness and thinness can be applied to any of the textures. Even a monophonic texture can be thickened by adding octave doubling, or thinned by reducing the sonority to a single line. Sudden change from thick to thin brings about a feeling of relaxed clarity and pleasant surprise. Sudden change from thin to thick brings both surprise and excitement (as in the overtures of Weber). Debussy creates *crescendi* and *diminuendi* by gradually adding or taking away various instruments.

In general, however, the problem is to create a relaxed variety of thickness and thinness of texture that is fitting to each kaleidoscopic change of musical mood. The *Brandenburg Concerti* by Bach illustrate the application of such variety to polyphonic texture. In certain movements of these *concerti* the rhythmic and motival unity is so intense that variety through light and shade is a natural necessity; Bach takes advantage of this organic need by creating a marvel of "cameo-like" variation in the number of voices.

SUFFICIENT VARIETY WITHIN GENERAL DESIGN

Maintenance of structural attractiveness depends upon sufficient variety in the organizational plan. A too long-continued use of any one general plan, when applied to contiguous segments of form, will cause monotony. There are four prototypical organizations which can be alternated to prevent this. Beethoven's music is the best source for illustration of such prototypes in creative action. His scores show an alternation of four basic organizational plans. These are shown on p. 280–281.

Such a balanced relation in structural organization may be defined as *normal alternation of organizational prototypes.*

Study as many scores as you can, to become familiar with this principle. Every composer must use some degree of variety

from BACH: *Brandenburg Concerto No. 5 in D Major* (By permission of Universal Edition A.G., Vienna)

PLATE XLV. VARIED THICKNESS AND THINNESS OF TEXTURE

279

TABLE V

(1) Monophonic statement	(unison line)
(2) Twofold organization	(woodwinds and strings in supplementary contrast)
(3) Oneness of organization of harmony and design	(full orchestra with only one melodic component strongly doubled)
(4) Antiphonal organization	(alternation of entry of choirs)

within general design. Study the symphonies of Beethoven particularly. He, more than any other composer, proved the classic strength of this procedure.

Four excerpts from Beethoven's *Symphony No. 6* illustrate these four types of prototypical organization:

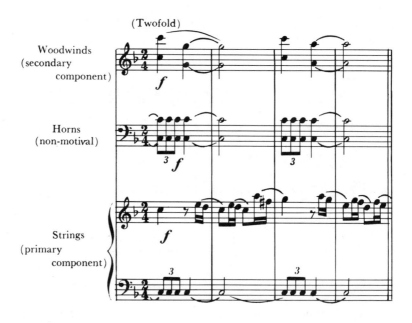

(Monophonic)

(Full orchestra with one melodic component)

281

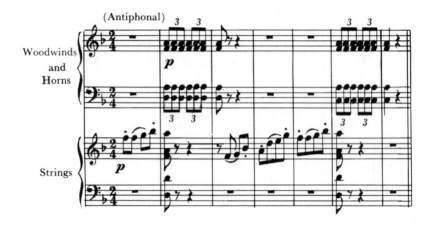

Another good illustration of the normal alternation of organizational prototypes is to be found in the *Symphony No. 4* by Brahms. At the beginning of the slow movement (page 64, Kalmus Edition) the first few measures are monophonic. These are followed by a oneness of organization of harmony and design (one melodic component), in which the woodwind and horn theme is doubled by the *pizzicato* strings. At measure 15 a twofold organization appears (two supplementary melodic components); this is followed by a return of the "onefold" statement. At measure 36 a striking antiphonal passage enters the scene. A study of this sequence of organizational prototypes will supply a clear and inspired example of balanced use.

Study other scores, particularly recent ones, to observe the continuing vitality of this stabilizing principle (normal alternation of organizational prototypes).

5

Orchestral
Types

*T*HE COMPOSER MAY BE EITHER EXPERIMENTAL OR
traditional in his choice of instrumentation. In either
case, it will be valuable to have in mind some knowledge of
the history of the orchestra and the evolution of the standard
instrumentations.

The earliest instrumental groups were probably random sets
of instruments which accompanied dancing or singing. There
was no standard orchestral instrumentation inherited from
earlier centuries. At the time of Bach and his contemporaries
(1700–1750), the *concerto grosso* type of instrumentation was
established. This orchestral ensemble included a body of accompanimental strings, a few featured solo instruments, and
the plectrum sound of the harpsichord. .

Haydn's period (1750–1800) crystallized the orchestra into
its classic division of three major families of sound: woodwind,
brass and strings. In Haydn's orchestra the woodwinds were
in pairs (two flutes, two oboes, two clarinets, two bassoons) and
the brass was limited to two natural horns and two natural
trumpets (without valves).

from BACH: *Brandenburg Concerto No. 2 in F Major* (Kalmus)

J. S. Bach
(1685 - 1750)

PLATE XLVI. THE PRE-CLASSIC OR BAROQUE ORCHESTRA

from HAYDN: *Symphony No. 94 in G Major, "Surprise"* (Kalmus)

Joseph Haydn
(1732-1809)

PLATE XLVII. THE CLASSICAL ORCHESTRA

from PROKOFIEV: *Classical Symphony in D Major* (Copyright 1926 by Editions Russe de Musique—reprinted by permission of Boosey & Hawkes, Inc., assignees of the copyright; also by permission of Kalmus)

PLATE XLVIII. THE CLASSICAL ORCHESTRA USED BY A 20TH-CENTURY COMPOSER

The Romantic Period (1800–1850) added the standard brass grouping (four horns, two trumpets and three trombones), and in the late Romantic Period (1850–1900) Wagner expanded the woodwinds to groups of three (three flutes, two oboes and cor anglais, two clarinets and brass clarinet, three bassoons). He also experimented with the addition of various types of tubas. In the music of Wagner the French horn came into its own with the invention of the valves, and brought in new melodic possibilities. Berlioz, in the early Romantic Period, was a great innovator who introduced many special effects, such as muted strings, valve cornets, harps, and strings *pizzicato*, and began a tendency toward "gigantism" which continued until Schönberg's *Gurre-Lieder* with its mammoth instrumentation (ten horns, for instance).

The next major development in orchestral instrumentation came from Russia in the late nineteenth century, through the music of Tchaikovsky, Rimsky-Korsakov, and—eventually— Stravinsky. The orchestra was not significantly expanded by these composers, except in certain works by Stravinsky which demanded larger brass and woodwind resources. What these composers were most significant for was their pioneering of a new consciousness of the vitality of tone color and instrumental motion, and for an emphasis on instrumental action for its own sake.

Debussy and the other "Impressionists" brought a new development to orchestration by putting the strings into the background and bringing the woodwinds into the foreground. They also gave new life and motion to the brass designs, and established the harp as an indispensable part of the total timbre. The reappearance of the "plectrum" sound supplied by the harp brought back into music an ingredient that had formerly been supplied by the harpsichord.

Today, all of the orchestral types mentioned in this short historical survey continue to influence composers to some degree, but the most recent tendencies are toward smaller, more varied,

from VAUGHAN WILLIAMS: *Symphony No. 4 in F minor* (Copyright in U.S.A. and all countries, 1935, by the Oxford University Press, London)

R. VAUGHAN WILLIAMS

PLATE XLIX. THE MODERN ORCHESTRA

from STRAVINSKY: *Le Sacre du printemps* (Copyright 1921 by Editions Russe de Musique; copyright assigned Boosey & Hawkes 1947—reprinted by permission)

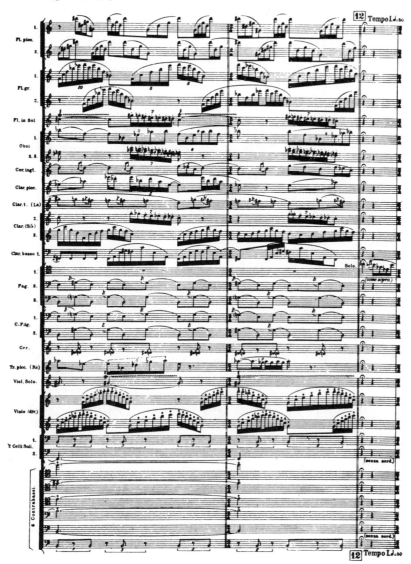

PLATE L. THE EXPANDED ORCHESTRA

289

from MILHAUD: *Symphony No. 1 for Small Orchestra,* "Le Printemps" (Universal)

Darius Milhaud.
1917.

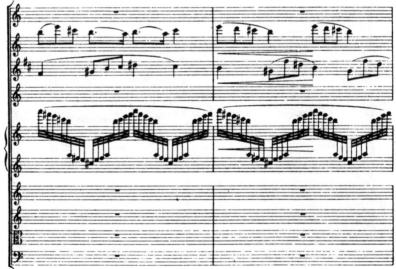

PLATE LI. THE CHAMBER ORCHESTRA

and intensely clear groups. Villa-Lobos, in Brazil, set an example by using very unusual groups of instruments, with the instrumentation constantly varied to suit the meaning of the composition or the adventurous interest of the composer. A tendency among the imitators of Webern, and exemplified by Pierre Boulez, is the use of small groups which contain almost the total mixture of basic tonal ingredients.

The American jazz groups have also added to the history of instrumentation. Worthy of notice are certain extended brass and woodwind ranges, the several brass mutes, new percussion effects, novel small and experimental combinations of instruments, and a certain textural fantasy that results from gifted improvisation.

Appendix A

THE 21 MEASURES IN THE EXAMPLE BELOW ILLUSTRATE instrumentation for a typical small laboratory ensemble of the type recommended for the 35 projects listed in this book.

These 21 measures also furnish a concentrated exercise in analysis, and show how it is possible to illustrate a large number of basic principles in one exercise.

TABLE VI

Measure	Principle
1	Punctuation and Heterophonic Unison
1–5	Contrast of Extreme Registers (high clarinet followed by low horn)
1–3	Contrast of *Staccato* and *Legato* (horizontal)
5–6	Pointillism
6–11	Overlapping
1–21	Restriction of Harmony (thin harmony throughout)
16–17	Unison for Power
	Monophonic Texture
19–21	Contrast of Timbre (antiphonal)
7–11	Homophonic Texture
9–11	Total Mixture (non-doubled)
14	Instrumental Activity
9–11	Polyphony
7–15	Unit Consistency (two-voice units—in strings and horns)
19–21	Motion as a Sustaining Factor
16–18	Contrast of Articulation

TABLE VI (*Cont.*)

Measure	Principle
7–15	Strings as Background
5–6	Percussion as a Sustaining Factor
7–15	*Staccato* and *Legato* in Contrast (vertical)
1–21	Normal Alternation of Organizational Prototypes (monophonic 1–4, twofold 7–11, "onefold" 16–18, antiphonal 19–21)

Locate these several specific illustrations, and analyze them for use of the principles indicated in Table VI.

Appendix B

Examples for Reference

A MOST IMPORTANT PART OF ORCHESTRATION STUDY IS the examination of scores to analyze the orchestration techniques of outstanding composers. The three charts which follow list numerous examples of the use of basic principles, systematically arranged to supply several examples of each principle. To find the page number for an example, first locate the column listing the principle in which you are interested. At the point where this column converges with the column listing the composer, you will find the specific page number.

The miniature scores chosen for this list are all standard works which should be obtainable in most music libraries. To ensure uniformity of page reference, all scores are E. F. Kalmus editions. The charts refer to examples from these scores.

TABLE VII

Bach	*Brandenburg Concerto No. 5 in D Major*
Haydn	*Symphony No. 101 in D Major* ("The Clock")
Mozart	*Symphony No. 40 in G minor*
Beethoven	*Symphony No. 8 in F Major*
von Weber	*Oberon Overture*
Berlioz	*Symphonie fantastique*
Schumann	*Symphony No. 1 in Bb Major* ("Spring")
Brahms	*Symphony No. 4 in E minor*
Wagner	*Tristan und Isolde* (Prelude and "Isolde's Love Death")
Tchaikovsky	*Symphony No. 6 in B minor* ("Pathétique")
Rimsky-Korsakov	*Scheherazade*
Debussy	*Prélude à L'après-midi d'un faune*
Stravinsky	*Petrouchka*

TABLE VIII

	Bach	Haydn	Mozart	Beethoven	von Weber	Berlioz	Schumann	Brahms	Wagner	Tchaikovsky	Rimsky-Korsakov	Debussy	Stravinsky
One-Voice Unit	—	25	—	—	—	133	—	64	—	72	154	1	51
Two-Voice Unit	51	24	57	3	19	139	25	109	—	38	74	—	7
Three-Voice Unit	10	12	45	—	—	159	—	125	3	122	13	23	113
Multiple Unit	—	—	—	46	—	165	—	—	33	168	—	27	—
Monophonic	—	47	54	—	—	100	—	64	—	29	154	1	41
Chordal	—	41	9	45	24	94	63	91	2	195	202	31	14
Polyphonic	34	65	42	—	—	35	—	145	8	215	—	—	—
Homophonic	13	28	3	57	16	63	77	1	40	96	50	3	89
Polythematic	39	31	41	104	20	205	15	111	—	40	—	13	131
Polyrhythmic	17	—	—	—	—	47	71	156	—	54	219	17	10
Heterophonic	—	—	99	10	—	207	117	79	—	50	209	27	85
Onomatopoeic	—	24	—	55	—	178	—	—	—	180	243	7	22
Pitch Distribution	—	14	37	104	11	167	6	127	—	190	75	10	115
Harmonic Limitation	—	14	41	75	21	177	61	131	—	86	70	11	87
Vivid Timbre	—	24	29	46	2	171	6	111	1	214	30	9	90
Two Components	48	32	34	33	22	71	31	111	12	72	180	13	131
Control of Dynamics	—	—	—	—	20	70	4	129	13	32	146	28	53

TABLE IX

	Bach	Haydn	Mozart	Beethoven	von Weber	Berlioz	Schumann	Brahms	Wagner	Tchaikovsky	Rimsky-Korsakov	Debussy	Stravinsky
Antiphonal Contrast	25	47	37	49	11	156	88	155	5	159	32	23	63
Instrumental Activity (flurry of motion)	30	29	—	56	2	121	76	137	12	180	139	23	99
Doubling for Power	1	41	41	33	35	151	112	109	15	197	200	18	44
Timbre Blend	9	24	—	64	—	71	68	65	—	77	171	29	80
Contrasted Pitch	—	31	—	50	—	22	49	—	—	170	84	9	115
Blend of Differentiated Motion	—	39	2	99	33	41	32	—	21	58	209	18	53
Extreme Registers	—	—	—	—	—	131	—	—	—	71	83	—	115
Contrasted Articulation	17	24	11	46	—	51	71	64	—	80	187	9	88
Overlapping	53	35	5	37	19	105	84	3	1	11	—	20	155
Pointillism	—	—	29	50	—	179	84	73	—	130	—	9	43
Total Mixture	—	—	—	—	—	—	—	—	—	—	—	17	12
Chord and Line	—	15	—	46	—	25	—	25	—	213	—	14	—
Motion as a Sustaining Factor	15	31	57	1	—	101	158	165	—	178	84	3	125
Percussion as Background	—	—	—	—	—	134	—	115	—	96	118	—	83
Strings as Background	—	45	—	75	—	101	33	48	49	22	86	27	89
Punctuation	—	25	11	51	21	158	47	153	2	140	177	25	51
Balance of Idiomatic Characteristics	—	29	11	41	17	143	52	134	45	25	192	27	65
Staccato and Legato (consecutive)	47	44	11	65	36	90	47	87	—	95	—	—	55
Staccato and Legato (simultaneous)	3	29	17	37	20	117	71	64	—	79	28	26	42
Expanded Tonal Groups	—	—	—	—	—	160	—	—	50	—	—	27	136

Bibliography

1. *Pedagogical books which are obsolescent but of interest to students of music history:*

   Gevaert, François Auguste, *New Treatise on Instrumentation.* Paris: Lemoine, 1895.

   Hoffman, Richard, *Practical Instrumentation.* New York: G. Schirmer, Inc., 1893.

   Prout, Ebenezer, *The Orchestra.* London: Augener, 1899.

   Widor, Charles-Marie, *The Technique of the Modern Orchestra.* London: Joseph Williams, 1906.

2. *Books which are of importance to formulation of general theories of orchestration:*

   Berlioz-Strauss, *Treatise on Instrumentation and Modern Orchestration.* New York: E. F. Kalmus, 1948.

   Ekman, Karl, *Jean Sibelius, His Life and Personality.* New York, Alfred A. Knopf, Inc., 1939.

   Guiraud, Ernest, *Traité Pratique d'Instrumentation.* Paris: Durand, 1933.

   Kohs, Ellis B., "An Aural Approach to Orchestration," *The Musical Mercury,* Vol. VI, No. 3–4 (March, 1939). New York: E. F. Kalmus.

Malipiero, Gian Francesco, *The Orchestra*. London: Chester, 1921.

Piston, Walter, *Orchestration*. New York: W. W. Norton & Company, Inc., 1955.

Rimsky-Korsakov, Nicolas, *Principles of Orchestration*. Berlin and New York: Edition Russe de Musique, 1923.

Rogers, Bernard, *The Art of Orchestration*. New York: Appleton-Century-Crofts, Inc., 1951.

Schillinger, Joseph, *The Schillinger System of Musical Composition*, Book XII, "Theory of Orchestration." New York: Carl Fischer, Inc., 1941.

Stravinsky, Igor, *The Poetics of Music in the Form of Six Lessons*. Cambridge: Harvard University Press, 1947.

Wagner, Richard, *On Conducting*. London: William Reeves, 1919.

Wellesz, *Die Neue Instrumentation*. Berlin: M. Hesse, 1929.

3. *Books which contain encyclopedic discussion of instrumentation*:

Forsyth, Cecil, *Orchestration*. New York: The Macmillan Co., 1935.

Read, Gardner, *Thesaurus of Orchestral Devices*. New York: Pitman Publishing Corp., 1953.

4. *Recent books with pedagogical emphasis*:

Anderson, Arthur Olaf, *Practical Orchestration*. Boston: C. C. Birchard, 1929.

Heacox, Arthur, *Project Lessons in Orchestration*. Philadelphia: Oliver Ditson, 1928.

Jacob, Gordon, *Orchestral Technique*. London: Oxford University Press, 1931.

Kennan, Kent Wheeler, *The Technique of Orchestration*. Englewood Cliffs, N. J.: Prentice-Hall, Inc., 1952.

Wagner, Joseph, *Orchestration: A Practical Handbook*. New York: McGraw-Hill Book Co., Inc., 1959.

5. *Books on the history of the orchestra and its instrumentation*:

Bekker, Paul, *The Story of the Orchestra*. New York: W. W. Norton & Company, Inc., 1936.

Carse, Adam, *The Orchestra in the Eighteenth Century*. Cambridge, England: W. Heffer and Sons, Ltd., 1940.

Carse, Adam, *The Orchestra from Beethoven to Berlioz*. Cambridge, England: W. Heffer and Sons, Ltd., 1948.

Carse, Adam, *The History of Orchestration*. London: Kegan Paul, Trench, Triebner and Co., Ltd., 1925.

Geiringer, Karl, *Musical Instruments, Their History from the Stone Age to the Present Day*. New York: Oxford University Press, Inc., 1945.

Sachs, Curt, *The History of Musical Instruments*. New York: W. W. Norton & Company, Inc., 1940.

General Index

GENERAL INDEX

Bartók:
  clarity, 106
  homophonic texture, 146
  instruments illustrated, 105
  string quartets, 97
  total mixture, 266
Bass:
  articulation, 100
  bowing, 101
  doubling, 100
  harmony, 100
  pizzicato, 100
  range, 100
  registers, 100
  timbre, 100
  transposition, 100
Bass clarinet:
  articulation, 37
  limitations, 36
  pitch, 36
  range, 32
  registers, 35
  scoring, 34
  timbre, 36
  transposition, 36
Bass drum, timbre, 69
Bass oboe, 31
Bassoon:
  articulation, 39
  blending, 41
  doubling, 41
  legato, 39
  limitations, 39
  motion, 41
  muted tone, 40
  skips, 39
  staccato, 39
  range, 39
  registers, 39
  technic, 41
  timbre, 41
Beethoven:
  alternation, 278
  bassoon, 40
  chordal texture, 131,
  clarity, 182
  doubling, 101,
  harmonic limitation, 169
  harmony, 171
  heterophonic texture, 147
  innovation, 264
  melodic components, 182, 189-91
  organization, 280
  spacing, 131
  staccato-legato 254
  string quartets, 97

Beethoven *(Cont.):*
  trumpet, 59
Bell-toned percussion, 222
Berio, electronic instruments, 260
Berlioz:
  antiphonal effects, 199, 201
  innovation, 264
  instrumentation, 287
  motion, 149
  pitch locale, 210
  spacing, 131
Bizet.
  cornet, 46
  heterophony, 158
  oboe, 28
  saxophone, 44
Blacher overlapping, 227
Blend:
  articulation, 221
  differentiated motion, 215
  doubling
    exact, 209
    octave, 209
  subtlety, 208
  timbre, 209
Bloch, 98, 100, 244
Boehm system, 12, 242
Boléro (Ravel), 44
Bongos, 79
Boulez, instrumentation, 268, 291
Bouncing bow (see *spiccato, saltato*)
Bowing:
  accent, 85-87
  alternation, 85-87
  anacrusis, 85-87
  bows per measure, 85-87
  cello, 99
  classic, 254
  col legno, 94
  détaché, 94
  down bows, successive, 86
  flautando, 94
  markings, 85-87
  martele, 93
  phrasing, 85-87
  ponticello, 94
  ricochet, 93
  rules, 85-87
  saltato, 93
  slur, 85-87
  spiccato, 93
  staccato, 93
  string bass, 101
  sul tasto, 94
  up bows, successive, 87

308

GENERAL INDEX

Concerto for Orchestra (Kodály), 141
Concerto for Two String Orchestras (Martinu), 260
Concerto No. 7 (Hovhaness), 223
Concertos:
  cello, 100
  violin, 97
Concierto de Aranjuez (Rodrigo), 83
Consistency: (of units)
  harmony, 107-108
  rhythm, 107-108
  rules, 107-108
Contra-bassoon:
  doubling, 42
  dramatic characterization, 42
Contrary motion, 173
Contrast:
  architectural elements, 147
  articulation, 221
  chord and line, 233
  homophonic texture, 142
  legato, 251, 255
  motive, 145
  pitch locale, 166, 214
  polythematism, 148
  staccato, 251, 255
  timbre, 109, 198, 208
    (table) 177
  tonal interest, 197
Copland, 33
  E flat clarinet, 33
  harmony, 175
Cor Anglais (see English horn)
Cornet:
  contour, 45-47
  timbre, 45-47
Counter-melody, 144
Craft, Robert, total mixture, 131
Cymbals:
  dynamics, 67, 69
  effects, 67, 69

Dance band (see Jazz)
Dance Rhapsody, A, (Delius), 28, 31
Danse macabre (Saint-Saëns), 41, 258
Danses sacrée et profane (Debussy), 82
Daphnis et Chloé (Ravel), 13, 244, 272, 276
Debussy:
  clarinet, 33
  doubling, 204, 208
  flute, 21
  harp, 82, 244

Debussy *(Cont.):*
  heterophony, 217
  homophony, 142
  idiomatic invention, 202
  impressionism, 226, 228, 242
  innovation, 264
  instrumentation, 287
  motion, 149
  non-extreme register, 220
  pitch distribution, 168
  pointillism, 226
  polyrhythm, 149
  thickness-thinness, 278
  timbre, 197
  voices, 170
  woodwind, 13
Delius
  bass oboe, 28
  harmony, 174
  heckelphone, 31
  legato, 255
  onomatopoeia, 158
  sarrusophone, 31
Deserts (Varèse), 271
Design:
  alternation, 102
  arpeggiation, 101
  combination, 103
  development, 102
  expansion, 102
  importance, 173
  "keel" action, 173
  light and shade, 278
  overlapping, 223
  rhythm, 101
  skips, 102
  thickness-thinness, 278
  wave pattern, 101
  values, 276
  variegation, 276-279
  vigor, 276-279
Détaché, 92, 251
Differences (Berio), 260
Differentiation:
  blend, 215
  homophonic texture, 142
  motion, 215
  polythematism, 145
Dissonance:
  contrast, 237
  percussion, 220
Distribution:
  harmony, 107-124, 165, 169
    (table) 172
  pitch, 165

GENERAL INDEX

Instruments *(Cont.):*
  cymbals, 69
  English horn, 29
  flügelhorn, 57
  flute, 20
  glockenspiel, 76, 205
  guitar, 82
  Hammond organ, 269
  harp, 81-83
  harpsichord, 80
  heckelphone, 31
  horn, 52-55
  lute, 233
  mandolin, 233
  marimba, 78
  oboe, 24
  oboe *d'amore,* 30
  Ondes Martenot, 269
  organ, 177, 269
  piano, 79, 205
  piccolo, 18
  plectrum, 80, 210
  rattle, 177
  sarrusophone, 31
  saxophone, 43
  snare drum, 68
  string bass, 100
  tambourine, 70
  tape recorder, 268
  tenor tuba, 64, 260
  theremin, 269
  timpani, 72-75, 192, 269
  triangle, 72
  trombone, 60-62
  trumpet, 56-59
  tuba, 63
  tubular bells, 78
  vibraphone, 78
  viola, 97
  viola *da gamba,* 12
  violin, 95, 96
  voices, human, 177, 270
  wood block, 71
  xylophone, 71, 205
Italian orchestras, early, 233

Janáček:
  clarinet, 33
  onomatopoeia, 161
Jazz:
  instrumentation, 268, 291
  mutes, 51, 59
  percussion, 242
  polyrhythm, 151

"Keel" action, design, 173
Key signatures, transposition of, 9
Kinaesthetic response:
  instrumental motion, 101
  polyrhythm, 151
Kodály, polyphony, 141

Leaps (see Skips)
Legato:
  bassoon, 39
  brass, 45, 51
  clarinet, 32
  contrast, 251-255
  flute, 15
  horn, 55
  markings, 14, 15
  oboe, 24
  piccolo, 14
  string bass 85-87, 100
  strings, 85-87
  trombone, 62
  trumpet, 58
  violin, 85-87, 96
  woodwinds, 14, 15
Leonore Overture No. 3 (Beethoven),
  off-stage trumpets, 59, 113
Lieutenant Kijé (Prokofiev):
  heterophony, 158-160
  saxophone, 43
Light and shade:
  design, 277
  overlapping, 224
Limitations:
  bass, 100
  bass clarinet, 36
  bassoon, 39
  bell sounds, 222
  brass, 45-50
  cello, 99
  clarinet, 35
  contra-bassoon, 42
  double bass, 100
  extreme register, 166
  flute, 22
  harmony, 169
  harp, 81-82
  harpsichord, 80
  horn, 54
  melodic components, 179-188
  oboe, 28
  piccolo, 18
  saxophone, 43
  trombone, 62
  trumpet, 58
  tuba, 64
  viola, 98

314

315

GENERAL INDEX

Mutes, brass:
    dynamics, 48
    harmonic background, 48
    horn, 54
    straight, 51
    timbre, 48, 58
    trumpet mutes, 51, 58

"Neptune" (see *Planets, The*)
Nineteenth Century:
    instrumentation, 210
    kinaesthetic values, 287
    polythematism, 148
Nutcracker Suite (Tchaikovsky):
    bass clarinet, 33
    differentiated motion, 215
    vivid timbre, 180

Oberon, Overture (Weber), 55, 301-303
Oblique motion, 173
Oboe:
    accompaniment, 24
    articulation, 24
    attack, 27
    bass oboe, 28
    extremes, 25, 26
    flutter-tongue, 27
    legato, 26
    limitations, 24-26
    muted tone, 27
    normal register, 24, 25
    range, 24
    registers, 25
    skips, 24
    staccato, 24
    timbre, 28
    trill, 26
Oboe *d'amore,* 30
Octandre (Varèse), 231
Octave doubling, (see Doubling)
Off-stage, antiphonality, 199
Ondes Martenot, 269
On Hearing the First Cuckoo in Spring (Delius), 158
Onomatopoeic texture:
    definition, 161
    diagram, 126
Orchestral types:
    illustration, 283
    recent trends, 291
Organ:
    Hammond, 269
    timbre, 177

Organization:
    prototypes of, 279
        (table), 281
Oriental music:
    articulation, 222
    monophonic texture, 129
    percussion, 265
    studies, 266
Ostinato, rhythmic, 240
Overlapping:
    definition, 224
    design, 275-277
    diagram, 225
    illustration, 227
Overtones, harmony, 169

Pacific 231 (Honegger), realism, 161
Paradiddle, 67
Parallel motion, 173
Parsifal (Wagner), 59
Pastoral Symphony (Vaughan Williams), 270
Pastorale d'été (Honegger), 55
Pedal timpani, 75
Pedals, harp, 81
Peer Gynt (Grieg) 21
Percussion:
    articulation, 222
    background, 240
    bell-tone, 76-80, 205
    dynamics, 67
    effects, 67
    experimentation, 265
    history, 265
    homophonic texture, 144
    markings, 67
    noise makers, 266
    patterns, 66
    piano, 80
    punctuation, 66
    purposes, 66
    ranges (bell-tone), 76-80
    rhythm, 67
    scoring, 66
    timbre, 66, 178
    values, 66
Peter and the Wolf (Prokofiev), 161
Petite Symphonie Concertante (Martin), 80, 233
Petrouchka (Stravinsky), 13, 59, 80, 152, 202, 221, 301-303
Phrasing:
    in bowing, 85-87
    staccato-legato, 251-257

317

GENERAL INDEX

Ravel *(Cont.):*
  strings, 244
  timbre blend, 204, 213
  voices, 272
  woodwinds, 13
Realism:
  music "concrete", 268
  texture, 155-161
Registers:
  alto flute, 23
  bassoon, 40
  brass, blending of, 50
  cello, 99
  chart of, 3-6
  clarinets, 33
  cornet, 58
  distribution, 165
  English horn, 29
  extremes, 176, 218
  flute, 21
  horn, 53
  oboe, 26
  piccolo, 17
  saxophone, 44
  strings, 95
  timbre, 198
  timpani, 73
  trombone, 61
  trumpet, 58
  tuba, 64
  variegation, 128
  viola, 98
  violin, 95
Renaissance composers, doubling, 210
Requiem (Berlioz), 199
Respighi:
  articulation, 224
  expanded brass, 260
  extreme registers, 220
  motion, 241
  onomatopoeia, 161
  pointillism, 239
Rhythm:
  chordal texture, 132
  consistency, 107
  patterns, 66
  percussion, 66
Rhythmic *ostinato,* 240
Ricochet, 93
Ride of the Valkyries (Wagner), 161
Rim shot, (see snare drum)
Rimsky-Korsakov:
  articulation, 223
  doubling, 204
  dynamic balance, 48

Rimsky-Korsakov *(Cont.):*
  homophonic differentiation, 142
  idiomatic invention, 200
  instrumentation, 287
  monophonic texture, 130
  motion, 149, 202
  reference chart, 301-303
  scale of intensities, 48
  trombone, 62
Robinson mute, 51
Rodrigo, guitar, 83
Roll (see snare drum)
Roll, drum, 67
Roman Festivals (Respighi), 161
Romantic Period:
  homophony, 142
  instrumentation, 287
  pitch locale, 167
  strings, 242
Romeo and Juliet Overture
  (Tchaikovsky), 207
"Ronde du Sabbat" (see *Symphonie fantastique*)
Roussel, instrumental motion, 203
Rubbra, polythematism, 150
Ruff (See snare drum)
Russian composers, instrumentation, 287
Russian Easter Overture (Rimsky-Korsakov), 62

Sacre du Printemps, Le (Stravinsky), 13, 41, 20, 202, 220, 289
Saint-Saëns:
  bassoon, 41
  cello, 100
  staccato-legato, 258
Salón México, El (Copland), 33
Saltato, 87, 93
"Saturn" (see *Planets, The*)
Saxophone:
  articulation, 44
  dramatic characterization, 44
  dynamics, 44
  harmony, 44
  limitations, 44
  range, 43
  registers, 44
  timbre, 44
  transposition, 44
  types, 44
Scarlatti, *staccato,* 255
Scheherazade (Rimsky-Korsakov), 130, 142, 202, 224, 301-303
Schelomo (Bloch) 100

318

Schönberg, instrumentation, 273, 287
Schubert, oboe, 28
Schumann:
  cello, 100
  chordal texture, 134
  flute, 23
  punctuation, 246
  reference chart, 301-303
Scoring, order of instruments, 11
Serenade for Tenor, Horn and Strings (Britten), 231
Shostakovitch, heterophony, 157
Sibelius:
  divisi strings, 260, 263
  harmony, 132
  idiomatic characteristics, 249
  polyphony, 226
  realism, 161
  strings, 260, 263
  sustained tone, 237
Siegfried Idyll (Wagner), 56
Sinfonia Concertante (Martinu), 219
Sinfonia India (Chávez), 265
"Sirènes" (see *Three Nocturnes*)
Six Lessons in the Poetics of Music (Stravinsky) 274
Skalkottas, instrumentation, 47
Skips:
  bassoon, 39
  clarinet, 32
  design, 103
  horn, 55
  oboe, 24
  violin, 96
Slur:
  bowing, 85-87, 251-256
  marking, 85-87, 251-256
Snare drum:
  dynamics, 67
  effects, 67
  flam, 68
  paraddidle, 68
  ratamacue, 68
  rimshot, 68
  roll, 68
  ruff, 68
  scoring, 66
Spacing:
  brass, 107-124, 131-137, 165-175
  chordal texture, 131-137
  harmony, 107-124, 131-137, 165-175
  horns, 118-120
  monophonic texture, 128

Spacing *(Cont.):*
  strings 107-124, 131-137, 165-175, 260
  woodwinds, 107-124, 131-137, 165-175, 259
Spectrum, 269
Spiccato, bowing, 87
Spider's Feast, The (Roussel), 203
Staccato:
  arpeggiation, 102
  bassoon, 39
  bowing, 85-87
  brass, 45, 51
  clarinet, 32, 37
  contrast, 251-255
  effects, 14, 51, 92-94
  flute, 14
  harp, 82
  harpsichord, 80
  horn, 53
  markings, 14, 15, 51, 92-94
  oboe, 24
  trombone, 62
  trumpet, 58
  tuba, 65
  violin, 92-94, 96
  woodwinds, 14, 15
Stockhausen, electronic music, 268
Stokowski:
  Bach transcription, 140
  polyphony, 140
Stopped horn, 54
Straight mute, 51
Strauss:
  E flat clarinet, 33
  horn, 55
  woodwinds, expanded, 262
Stravinsky:
  bassoon, 41
  clarity, 106
  heterophony, 217
  idiomatic invention, 62, 202
  instrumentation, 287
  motion, 62, 202
  piano, 80
  polyrhythm, 152
  reference chart, 301-303
  timbre, 197
  tonal interest, 197
  tradition, 274
  trumpet, 59
  woodwinds, 13
String bass (see Bass)
String effects, 92-94
String quartets, 97

319

GENERAL INDEX

String section:
  Beethoven, 169
  instrumentation, 11, 121-123, 260
  scoring, 11
  spacing, 121-123, 260
String sound, impressionism, 244
Strings:
  articulation, 221, 222, 249
  background, 243
  bowing, 85-87
  chords, 88
  divisi, 260
  dynamics, 193
  effects, 92-94
  expansion, 260
  harmonics, 90
  intervals, 88
  legato, 251
  markings, 85-87
  motion, 249
  pizzicato, 96-100
  ranges, 5-7
  registers, 5-7
  staccato, 251
  timbre, 98
  values, 84, 243, 249
Structure:
  design, 276
  idiomatic characteristics, 249
  "keel" action, 173
  light and shade, 277
  motion, 173
  overlapping, 277
  textures, 125-161
  thickness-thinness, 277
  tonal interest, 197
  values, 276-283
Studie im Pianissimo (Blacher), 227
Suite for Viola and Piano (Bloch), 98
Sul Tasto, 94
Sustained motion, 228, 240
Sustained sound, pointillism, 228
Sustained tone, 237
Sustaining elements, in homophony, 143
Sustaining factor, motion, 237
Swan of Tuonela, The (Sibelius), 260, 263
Symphonic band:
  instrumentation, 233
  timbre, 177
Symphonie fantastique (Berlioz), 47, 201, 216, 247, 301-303
Symphonie Miniature No. 2 (McKay), 63
Symphony No. 3 (Beethoven), 189

Symphony No. 4 (Beethoven), 190
Symphony No. 5 (Beethoven), 191
Symphony No. 6 (Beethoven), 147, 158, 169, 249, 254, 280-283
Symphony No. 7 (Beethoven), 131
Symphony No. 8 (Beethoven), 247, 301-303
Symphony No. 1 (Bizet), 28
Symphony No. 4 (Brahms), 283
Symphony No. 8 (Dvořák), 42, 252
Symphony No. 94 (Haydn), 285
Symphony No. 101 (Haydn), 301-303
Symphony in D minor (Franck), 46, 59, 164, 238, 260
Symphony No. 2 (Mahler), 195
Symphony No. 1 for Small Orchestra (Milhaud), 231, 291
Symphony No. 25 (Mozart), 256
Symphony No. 40 (Mozart), 301-303
Symphony No. 5 (Rubbra), 150
Symphony No. 1 (Schumann), 23, 134, 246, 301-303
Symphony No. 1 (Shostakovich), 157
Symphony No. 5 (Tachaikovsky), 55
Symphony No. 6 (Tachaikovsky), 301-303
Symphony No. 4 (Vaughan Williams), 288
Syntax, musical, 179

Tannhäuser (Wagner), 233
Tape recorder, 268
Tapiola (Sibelius), 161
Tchaikovsky:
  bass clarinet, 33
  brass, 62
  doubling, 207
  horn, 56
  instrumentation, 287
  pitch distribution, 215
  polythematism, 147
  reference chart, 301-303
  timbre blend, 208
  trombone, 62
  vividness, 180
Tenor tuba (see Baritone horn)
Terminology, musical, 178
Textural types, diagrams, 125-126
Texture:
  chordal, 131
  compound, 163
  definition, 125-126
  heterophony, 153

320

GENERAL INDEX

322